Iron Mountain Winter

Michael T. Ribble

Copyright © 2022 Michael T. Ribble

All rights reserved. No part of this book may be reproduced or transmitted in any form or by any means, electronic or mechanical, including photocopying, recording or by any information storage and retrieval system without permission in writing from the publisher.

Apalachicola – Dumfries, VA
ISBN: 978-1-7330842-4-6
eBook ISBN: 978-1-7330842-5-3
Library of Congress Control Number: 2022916306
Title: Iron Mountain Winter
Author: Michael T. Ribble
Digital distribution | 2022
Paperback | 2022

This is a work of fiction. The characters, names, and dialogue are products of the author's imagination, and are not to be construed as real.

Cover photo credit: Michael T. Ribble

Dedication

To:
Carroll Arnett (Gogisgi)
Lawrence J. Cece
Charles M. Westie
George A. Zorn
and most especially, Baerbel, my love and muse.

Other books by Michael T. Ribble

Lieutenant Jacob Starke and Calypso
Lieutenant Jacob Starke and the Anarchists
Lieutenant Jacob Starke and the Spanish Gunboats
Lieutenant Jacob Starke in Cuba

Table of Contents

Iron Mountain 1
Deep Winter 2
Upper Peninsula Pond 3
Girl to Woman 7
A Final Shopping Trip 8
Second Grade Recollections 9
Peregrinations 10
Menominee Fireflies 11
Afternoon at the Lake 12
Extinguished 13
Caught in the Draft..14
Country School in Summer..16
City of Elms 18
Below Asphalt..20
Three Monuments 23
First Blood 24
Requiem for a Lady 25
National Spotted Swine..26
A Sow Betrayed 28
Caring Intervention 29
A World of Cattle...30
Disquieting Quests 33
Youthful Arrogance 34
Suppression 35
Query Deferred 36
Eternal Hourglass...37
Perilous Befuddlement...38
Blind Prisoners...39
The Deluded Hipster 40
Bus Station Blues...41
Sharing the Ride..42
Passing Bus Windows..43
North Camp Twilight 44

The Final Redoubt	46
A Spectral Haven	48
Interstate Night	50
North to Boulder	52
The Hill Mythology	53
Aficionado	58
A Gentle Innocent	60
Getting Right	61
Rites of Spring '72	62
Transient Tolerance	69
Perpetual Resistance	70
Reflections	71
Redux in Black	72
Forty Acres and a Mule	73
Western Exile	74
Sangre de Cristo	75
Swan Song	80
Working Wounded	83
Eight-ball and a Quarter	84
Western Slope Sisters	87
Colorado Rounder	89
Fatal Misjudgments	91
Indigenous Expatriate	93
Hipster Redux	94
A Curious Epoch's Volunteers	97
Into the Bay	100
Evening Chimerical	101
The Last Port Call	104
Friends, Companions, and Shipmates	105
Paris Nocturne	106
Key West Adieu	107
A Mazatlán Night	108
Heilbronn Woods	109
A Dubious Hunt	111
The Green Glass Bowl	114
The Heretic	116
Humanity	117
A Place We've Never Been	118
Somewhere Out West	119

Street Philosopher's Demise	120
Late Summer Idyll	121
Beyond the Crossroad	122
A Spinster Aunt	124
Passages	129
Winter's Approach	130
Prelude	131
Incubus	132
Lewy Body	133
A Tenuous State	134
Sisyphus, Prometheus, and the Tourist	136
The Hemingway Organ	144
Through a Wyrd Portal	148
Seeing the Elephant	159
Acquiescence	166
At the Precipice	167
Crossing the Styx	168
Homage to a Line	169

Iron Mountain

Iron Mountain hugs Michigan's Upper Peninsula along the Wisconsin line. Henry Ford built auto bodies and gliders there from maple and birch forests; then factory, camps, and sawmills vanished. Weakening wood shoring deep below ground supports flooded mine shafts but far above this Stygian underworld are stores, small factories, a towering ski jump, Discalced Carmelites convent, and Veterans Hospital. Men that once flocked north across the straits by ferry, then bridge, to escape, drink, and hunt have disappeared with their factory jobs; leaving abandoned camps, idle bars, solitary cafes, and gas stations along lonely asphalt roads. Those dwelling there enjoy, tolerate, or endure saturated springs; ephemeral summers; and brief falls before winter's hermitic stillness melds real and surreal.

Deep Winter

Northern winter night,
frigid, still, and silent
with transient ghosts and biting cold.
Ice crust glistening on white snow;
pregnant with the next storm,
nourishing a keenness for spring;
that joyous harbinger,
of summer's tenuous warmth.

Upper Peninsula Pond

Down the northern forest lane,
a seldom-traveled, hard-packed track
winds between shifting sand shoulders.
Its hot, twisting, uneven crown
sparsely sprinkled with defiant green blades,
skirts one summer-still pond
before curving into a thinly grassed clearing
with summer cottage turnaround.

Second growth pine's tart odor,
golden-crowned green dandelions
scattered between brush, rock, and sand;
struggle to survive dry heat and sterile soil.
Small birds flit betwixt overhead needle nests
wedged in serene pine, maple, beech, and birch;
above chirping insects unable to evade ravenous birds,
while ants toil and war across their severe terrain.

Grasping, sucking mud below placid pond water
gently brushing a brief ribbon of sandy shore;
resisting the thin, hesitant grass mat
encircling a solitary summer cottage.
Water spiders striding a smooth surface;
unwary, reliant on habit, ignorance, and chance;
with their every disturbance inviting swift death,
from ahead, behind, below, or above.

Multi-colored, bi-winged dragon flies,
whether striking or mundane,
flutter between horsetail stalks.
Brown-bodied, sharp biting deer flies
with translucent blurring swept-back wings,

fly cover for sanguine mosquitoes;
lurking amidst dancing clouds
of white and pale-yellow butterflies.

The elegant wood-duck drake,
proud in exquisite plumage,
glides serenely through the tranquil pond
above frantic feet sowing glutinous fish eggs.
Minnows flash through warm shallows,
avoiding agile, brightly colored sunfish,
pedestrian bluegills, ravenous black crappies,
and flashing, streamlined yellow perch.
Pike, bass, bullheads, and catfish
cruise the deep, dark water further out;
loitering expectantly, impatient for the unsuspecting
or provender drifting down from above.

Life grows abundant in tepid shallows
gently caressing dark, decapitated stumps
rising from small, shallow, faux coves.
Green algae blooms brush the surface,
clinging to decaying wood, stripped of bark.
An ancient, gently-swaying, solitary willow,
overhangs the long-crushed steel spillway;
beside a rusting wheelbarrow frame
abandoned beneath shallow, lipid water.
Revealed when a tolerant sun permits;
its wood rotted away since discarding,
uncounted years past.

Translucent, warm water blankets and conceals
chilled layers where it deepens and darkens,
until flashing ice cold from the artesian spring;
replenishing water escaping down a small brook
flowing triumphantly from the southern bank;
rolling slowing over ghost-yellow crayfish,
past sunning black-shelled turtles
and beyond green frogs crouching in the afternoon sun.

The bottom's amorphous spongy mass
formed of debris, leaves, twigs, earth, entwined;
where muck and water become indistinguishable,
and a spring thinning winter ice five fathoms up.
Invisible in this frigid, dark preserve;
shadowy stacked timber rests silent,
lashed by rusting wrapping chains,
on the logging sled settling a hundred years;
its tongue angled up into blackness,
lifted by traces of bone, harness, collars,
two bells, and eight shoes calked with spikes;
all useless when late winter's ice crumbled
under two chestnut brown Belgium geldings;
pulled under in their traces, kicking and screaming;
until bubbles stopped surfacing through the fissure.

A young woman moves carefully with gentle purpose
to the rough, splintered dock resurrected each spring;
for sunning, fishing, a jon boat, and canoe.
She leaves the wood-framed summer cottage
built over an abandoned cook shack foundation,
with screened doors, glazed windows, clothesline,
and decaying plywood outhouse abandoned to wasps.
At the sagging dock's head, crude and rough;
this thin maiden with black-silk hair, damply glistening
against olive skin in high summer's heat
kicks off sandals, unbuttons faded jeans,
lets them fall, easily clearing thin swimmer's legs.
After tossing faded denim aside,
she crosses arms and the white blouse
lifts above her head to join the rest,
leaving white cotton panties,
exposing a flat belly below small breasts
proud above spreading female hips.

As though supplicating, she points hands,
then launches her sylphlike form;
piercing the pond's skin like a stiletto,
warm, cool, cold, then constant;

leaving no more than ripples.
She feels water invading her,
but continues deeper, darker, colder
before racing back to the sunlit surface.

In a practiced crawl, surging forward,
she cuts a slight, smooth wake
through this still, fertile, welcoming pond;
conscious of its entombed team,
from adolescence's summer nightmares;
but not their shadowy, unmarked grave.
They drowned before her mother's birth;
and safely distant from cabin where she was conceived.

Girl to Woman

Fields of fresh-mown hay,
rippled by spring's zephyr.
Meadows blooming green,
stirring white lace curtains,
shielding warm bedroom windows.

Flowers in a cut-glass vase,
green stems bent by clear water,
her rag quilt of many colors
draped over the brass footboard;
small things neatly placed;
aligned for her spring;
before summer then fall.

A Final Shopping Trip

Where's the Bisquick, grandmother?
You search the supermarket shelves
of your existential world.
Why look so hard? So resolute?
Such an easy quest;
but eyes are dull, body worn;
and you've earned a rest.

Second Grade Recollections

Small boys talking on a summer porch;
debating earliest memories.
The youngest evokes a red haze;
indescribable, warm, safe, and snug;
yet remains silent and listens;
unwilling to face ridicule, unable to explain.
A dream, a vision, a fragment, a delusion?
The red, brown, and blue plastic birds
tethered above cribs carry unanimously.

Peregrinations

Those passing crowded lives,
seek to relive repetitive flashes,
suffering through their addiction;
then pass away thirsty.

Those blessed with good lives,
even commonplace,
see intermittent flashes
of magic and mystery;
cherished until erasure.

Those leading pedestrian lives,
pass through circadian motions,
exist without disruption,
live without purpose;
but no better or no worse for it.

Menominee Fireflies

Warm midsummer evening,
moist, sparkling and still.
Its thousand winking lights
the fireflies filling June's ardent sky;
flittering over darkening meadows.

Predators seeking mates,
rising from trees and mud,
passing coded invites,
waiting longingly, expectantly,
to dance another cycle through.

A life passing amidst
fireflies' green luminescence
in the evening's soothing magic
should never end without
marveling at this minuet.

Their splendor nearly missed
until my time mostly passed;
but never did I ever
bottle a solitary firefly;
to that I must attest.

Afternoon at the Lake

The drab green Willys wagon parked in a graveled lot across the blacktop from a tavern he once owned at the lake; just feet from his compact bungalow. Grandmother brought grandson to her brother-in-law's sunlit bedroom; just enough for bed, nightstand, and dresser. While her husband confers with their lawyer she culls a life's remnants. After refusing a high school diploma on forgotten principle, he turned to things mechanical was chauffeur, mechanic, and motorcycle cop before the Great War. Over there, he led a company repairing vehicles, got tattooed, found another language, fell in love, and forced to return. Back home, his dog only answered French commands while he drank with comrades, soldiers, a Russian refugee, and artists. Tavern, hunting, and fishing filled his wants. He invested well when not drying out with the Sisters and resisted Prohibition as an abomination. His tavern was a clandestine and sophisticated haunt until repeal then local characters' habitué throughout the depression and another war. He married an athletic flapper and divorce did not disrupt their breakfasts; five cottages down the road. This rare life inexorably disintegrated until the good, kind, and popular man; a devoted son and indigenous expatriate, expired beneath his bedroom window in the same fine sand a great-nephew drags black tennis shoes through; bored with the errand and ignorant of his loss.

Extinguished

The doctor had two sons,
one became an engineer;
the other went to war.

The engineer had two sons,
one became an engineer,
the other went to war.

The engineer had a son,
who went to war;
and another line died out.

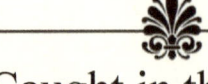
Caught in the Draft

Neighbors on the board
drafted the father at nineteen;
but not their sons, not those
destined for better things.

He fell in and toed the line;
marched to work,
marched to drill,
marched to sick call,
marched to movies.

He stood tall on parade
in an issue uniform;
no Eisenhower jacket;
no red cravat.
Berated by a colonel,
before discovering
he was the only issue soldier.
Alpha company passed a hat
then no issue soldiers paraded;
the captain's entire company
wore Eisenhower jackets
and red cravats.

He went by troopship to Alaska,
heaving with the gently rolling sea,
living on soda crackers and tasteless water,
until they marched ashore.

He went on field maneuvers
with fixed bayonets;
to spear fat salmon

that replaced field rations.

He exercised with a heavy rifle,
flushing the tawny brown moose
soldiers were not allowed to shoot.
One dwarfing fleet Michigan whitetails,
attacked him and was shot up the ass;
but punishment detail quickly passed.

He was promoted corporal,
then busted for not sewing on another stripe;
useless for the verdant dairy farm and family,
anxiously awaiting his return.

Two years and honorable discharge,
beyond the reach of neighbors' board,
eschewing their pampered, protected ones;
back at home with wife and son,
he faced what was to come, his duty done.

Country School in Summer

Five miles to town, off hot blacktop,
a campus encircled by field corn and alfalfa;
quiet, so very quiet; hot, still, and dusty.
Parched grass, still fresh-mown
to the taut woven-wire fence.
Square, red-brick building; rising solemnly
above pea-stone gravel encircling a white flagpole;
its limp ropes wrapped round steel
since nothing flies in August.

Concrete steps rise to a silent building,
without children, without teachers,
without stiff, brown, lunch bags.
No gaudy lunch boxes
lining its center stairwell,
rising to second floor classrooms.
Basement for kindergarteners,
main floor for first-graders,
top level for second-graders;
when promoted.

Brown grasshoppers whirr below a gliding blackbird;
red feathers paused as keen eyes scour short grass.
One white butterfly flutters about tall, shaded windows,
opening on a wood floor under rows of varnished oak desks
with vestigial inkwells and cast iron frames.
Black slate sections hanging over their long, dusty chalk tray
dominate the front wall below a green cursive alphabet.
The teacher's ponderous desk and lifeless flag fill one corner;
across from a closet of hardcover texts, used and marked up;
stacked below shelves of brown cardboard boxes;
overflowing with chalk, crayons, paste, and paper.

Small, unshaded basement windows
pierce its poured concrete foundation;
overlooking tables, storybooks, and toys;
well-ordered piles in mute repose
like the outside playground equipment.
Galvanized pipes of swing sets
tower above unmoving, dangling chain links;
their steel claws holding thick canvas-rubber seats
suspended over bald spots slowly yielding to grass.
Wood-plank teeter-totters under layers of thick paint
left angled across thick, steel fulcrum-rods.

Every August passes hot and silent;
yielding to a virgin September,
bringing the next school year and one-floor rise.
Newbie basement denizens start their climb
to the first floor, then second;
and finally off to town.

Study, talk, brag, play, debate, and wrestle;
then eat lunch with sandwiches pulled from brown bags;
waxed milk cartons pierced by paper straws;
or gaily colored lunch buckets with thermos.

Vibrant through fall, winter, and spring;
before another summer cloaks this building
in still, sultry solitude along hot country blacktop,
five miles from town, amidst field corn and alfalfa.

City of Elms

The small Midwest farm town; dawning city
where American elms overhang paved streets,
line banks of its chocolate-brown river
slowly twisting through freshly mown parks;
shading back-yards, front-yards, and parking lots;
arcing over streets and gravel roads;
spreading across fields and woodlots;
surrounding monumented cemeteries.

Beau idéal of trees with green canopies.
Loved, sought, popular, plentiful.
Favored for the artist's canvas.
Gilding fall's ground with leaves,
above hand-clasped roots
entwined in underground communities.

Generations blossom in muddy spring,
flourish in summer's sun and storms,
shed leaves and gather sap in fall,
repose during Indian summer,
then endure winter's cold aura
and ice-coated snow.

Devastated by a foreign plague;
beetle-borne decimation
destroyed this green community,
tree by tree by tree by tree by tree.
Chains rip through bark to heartwood;
felled then dragged to burn piles,
or left skeletal in forests and fields;
white sentinels among the living.

Burned or rotted away,
generations come and go,
American elms live in books,
in pictures, in memories;
but not on the land,
and that Midwest city
is no longer of the elms.

Below Asphalt

Behind main street's disparate red-brick stores,
beneath parking lots' tacky summer asphalt,
under the cold winter's frozen surface,
covered by fall's whirling leaves and trash,
blemished with oil stains, skid marks, and paint;
lies a buried past not acknowledged.

On a slope, long since leveled,
on half of a half of a city block
sat the doctor's house;
a young couple's wedding present,
below towering elms;
with backyard garden,
of flower beds, bushes,
sweet black-cherry trees,
and carriage horse paddock.

The almost, but not quite, flat roof
surrounded its solid brick chimney.
Two stories of chalking white siding
pierced by tall, four-pane windows,
with green louvered shutters.
Four blue-gray porches,
girded by carved white pillars,
and railings above flat lattice.

The doctor's bride gave him sons;
one to university the other to France.
Nights in their silent front parlor,
staring into a black-marble fireplace,
marking time until their soldier's return;
but not the same, never the same.

His brother took a schoolteacher bride,
then came five; two girls, two boys,
and the little one who died.

The aging doctor cared for patients,
in hospital, homes, and downstairs office.
Traveling by foot, sleigh, or carriage;
winter, summer, spring, and fall;
while his wife gave home remedies
over their wooden crank-phone in the hall.
Sunday's fishhooks, the Spanish Flu,
colds, births, and brakemen's amputations
continued until winter silenced him forever,
and his bride in early spring.

Basement rooms took their locked trunks,
Then came others crammed with clothes;
growing higher as the generation passed.
A driver filled the cistern with black coal;
cemented shut with a young daughter's
tiny handprint seal on its gritty border.
The coal room gained a fuel oil tank;
safely distant from the sons' clandestine still;
and root cellar where vegetables and swords
waited in cool darkness under a window sill.
Their horses finally hauled away;
surrey discarded, then the sleigh;
for a black Peerless cabriolet;
whose garage consumed stable and loft.

During another war,
the doctor's son and loving wife
no longer at the fireplace,
sat around a wood-sheathed wireless.
Their son off to fight in foreign lands,
a starving purgatory then return,
to a home no longer the same.

The backyard garden went to city hall;

trees, flowers, and paddock;
for a cyclone-fenced, blacktopped parking lot.
Their grown children went off;
leaving them to crosswords and *Saturday Evening Post*.
Passing nights together
by a square, flickering screen 'til late
with Lawrence Welk and Arthur Godfrey.
Welcoming family on Thanksgiving
with turkey, stuffing, and trimmings.
When his bride suddenly passed,
the old man refused to last.
Four long blocks of parking came,
as city merchants cleared house and grass.

Under that long blacktop expanse,
behind main street's disparate red-brick stores;
beneath spring's hesitant thaw,
beneath summer's tacky asphalt,
beneath winter's frozen ground,
beneath fall's multicolored leaves,
beneath oil, rubber, and paint;
these ghosts thought of not at all.

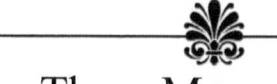

Three Monuments

The midday sun glints from perhaps a half-dozen headstones outside a small main street shop. All blank save one with a ten-year-old boy's name and dates carved precisely in polished black granite. A solemn couple paying their bill learn it was retrieved from his grave for display when the mother could not pay.

The woman saw her own son's name on that glowing dark slab, and a mother's rage flared until her man paid for two; then warned the mason to return it before that boy's mother became aware. Neither knew woman, boy, or cemetery but it was her first show of spirit in six weeks.

First Blood

Concealed by the abandoned granary,
battered Red Ryder BB gun in hand
a young Orion stalks the swallow;
blue-winged with small, white breast,
perched on the cracked electric line,
sagging between broken, white insulators.

A coppered ball strikes its left wing.
Fluttering, falling, spinning, into dusty gravel;
its exposed wing bone glistening white.
A lovely swallow quivering, staggering,
unable to elude a stunned, sickened boy:
who always missed,
who collected the bird,
who made a cardboard cage,
who nursed it to death,
who cried while burying it;
stiff, lifeless, and unmoving,
in the neglected apple orchard.

Requiem for a Lady

Black and brown Border Collie puppy,
brought from the old woman's kennel;
for a boy who raised, fed, and stroked the bitch.
They ran together over fields and through woodlots
in winter's cold and summer's heat.
He watched four guinea-pig puppies emerge;
found her lifeless alongside the summer asphalt;
and cried as a dull shovel chipped at cement-hard clay,
to bury her in the burlap bag shroud;
blood-soaked and broken.

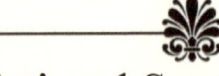

National Spotted Swine

Off the dusty, gravel road,
beyond a battered mailbox,
down the rutted dirt path,
through brush and trees;
wait haphazard pens and sheds
scattered about a cluttered clearing
below his one-room shack on rising ground.

A door above rough board stairs
opens to frugal lodgings
under bare rafters and cobwebs
with a tarnished tuba wedged between joists.
The dull brass bed and wood stove
dominate a space defined by tarpapered walls
with another life's fading snapshots.

His diminutive dwelling
surpasses downhill
sheds, pens, and crates.
In and around them are pregnant gilts;
and sows wading through squealing litters
of flat, wet noses, and needle-teeth seeking teats.
Nearby, shoats, swine, and hogs root through moist dirt;
confined to their fenced pasture and sparse lean-to;
bordering a swamp of drowned trees and stumps:
blanched, silent, still, and ringed by the living.

An old man ambles carefully forward,
long white hair, bib overhauls, patched clothes;
his austere life shared with National Spotted Swine;
no mixed breeds, chickens, or dogs.
Companions and family;

smart, content, and clean;
until his thrumming black Chevrolet pickup,
with dark-green pine racks
ornamented by hand-painted pig signs,
delivers them up to the stockyards.

A Sow Betrayed

The boy raised Bridget as his pet,
fed the gilt well and had her bred;
spent long nights in the farrowing shed.
Every litter ten and a runt; born alive
and never crushed in their crowded bed.

When farming passions cooled;
she was left free to wander,
never fenced, never strayed,
loved a scratch behind warm, floppy ears.
Coaxed up the ramp into a flat-rack truck;
scared but trusting after three contented years.
Slaughtered for a three-speed bicycle
finally left outside to rust away,
unlike the Judas guilt that remained.

Caring Intervention

Three foundered horses shared the shaded corner of a hundred acres with ponds and uncut alfalfa fields. Passing time beneath an oak tree's summer shade, scratching against woven wire, they eyed the occasional car, truck, or tractor roll down the gravel road on the other side; trailing a cloud of fine, brown dust. Hobbling over to a rusty wire fence, their large, wet lips and yellow teeth took apples from elated children.

Three foundered horses neighing protests were herded up the ramp into a closed truck after one city woman accused their owner of neglect. They were not like her geldings; boxed in solitary stalls until turned loose for an hour to nervously pace their exercise yard with painted white railings scalloped from nervous chewing.

Three foundered horses have gone. The lady lives content and righteous, her duty fulfilled. The slaughter house is finished, weeds blanket their hoof-marked refuge, and hundreds of grasshoppers replace cheerful whinnies only absent children remember.

A World of Cattle

Calves;
slip from the womb;
dropping to the ground
in a soggy, squirming heap;
lapped by a warm, rasping tongue;
clearing away trauma, blood, and mucus
until their silk-soft coat shines;
wet with pristine ignorance.
A fresh, virgin frame stands;
unsteady hind legs,
wobbly forelegs,
then startled, bawling head
searching for welcoming teats.

Cows;
offer soft, warm skin;
but a steel pail's white rubber
might instead reward ten months
curled in dark isolation.
A new life, about to face
heaven, hell, or purgatory;
within its destiny ordained
by market, mother, and herd.

Bull calves;
if allowed to remain so,
grow to be milked
but stud neither cow nor heifer.
Most are soon castrated,
transformed into steers.
Some penned in the dark,
fed wet, soggy slop,

then slaughtered for veal.
Some pass an idle life,
fattened in feedlots,
then slaughtered.
Some are fettered
to the heavy wood yoke,
for arduous service.
Few avoid slaughterhouse or knacker.

Heifer calves;
may become cows.
Some penned in the dark,
fed wet, soggy slop,
then slaughtered for veal.
Some pass an idle life,
fattened in feedlots
then slaughtered.
Some, impregnated by pipette,
birth many generations.
Some are kept lactating until dry.
Few avoid slaughterhouse or knacker.

Cattle's predestination awaits;
set by breed, birth, and custom.
Some as sacred wanderers;
like the gentle, skittish Zebu and Brahman.
Some bred for the arena;
fighting bulls, calming steers,
or cows birthing warriors.
Some live a life being milked:
black and white Holsteins for volume,
or Jersey and Guernsey for cream.
Some are fattened for their flesh;
ambrosial Angus or hardy Hereford
whose sole destiny is the slaughterhouse.
Some will fade into history,
like resilient, autonomous longhorns;
now spectral book and film visions.

Whether purebred or crossbreed:
living free, regimented, or in feedlots;
fed hay, grass, corn, or mash;
fought, milked, or eaten;
ungainly or fleet;
stolid or skittish;
docile or volatile;
curious or dull;
passive or aggressive;
exploited, feral, or pet;
horned or polled;
in pastures or on the plains;
crammed in pens or trucks;
revered or branded;
healthy or diseased;
all living unaware, unable to resist,
unknowingly bowing to their controllers.

Death comes;
slow or quick,
gentle or painful;
grass slope, pen, or killing chute.
Leaving their carcass
for the butcher,
for the grave,
for the renderer,
for back-forty scavengers and maggots.
Leaving a predestined existence
measured in milk, meat, leather, glue, fertilizer,
and circuses.

A singular few;
frightened, pet, or warrior,
kill their controllers with reason
but without understanding.

Disquieting Quests

Walking down the familiar road,
a wayfarer lurched slowly by;
clutching book and empty jug,
asking solemn pilgrims why?

None looked twice nor did reply;
not a single traveler stopped or slowed.
They looked to the sky or turned away;
walking quickly on with purpose,
fearing revival of some buried past,
and those mad enough to pry.

Youthful Arrogance

Give us:
a story, we'll listen;
a horse, we'll mount;
a road, we'll travel;
a wind, we'll sail;
a vice, we'll forsake;
a trespass, we'll embrace;
a cause, we'll support;
a diktat, we'll rebel.

Suppression

Lashed hard astride security's spar,
avoiding every threat;
never straying far afield,
from tales of gallant treks.

Bolting for security's ports,
mostly those just lately quit;
staring bold through colored glass,
at heroes never met.

Embracing security's alluring charm,
ignoring outward signs,
marking what I am;
that primeval, unsettling impulse
dormant in domesticated men.

Query Deferred

Where will I go when I die?
What will I do when I die?
Why should it matter?
today I am alive;
with no tomorrow promised.

Eternal Hourglass

Life's coarse, dry sand
sifts silently through fingers,
leaving a few remembered grains
of mutated, decaying memories;
until emptied.

Perilous Befuddlement

On a pilgrimage to the priest,
to question how and why;
he raised his hand,
rolled his eyes,
then bowed his head;
faith was the soft reply.
Ran back home to mother,
surely she must know,
but blushing kind and sweet,
could only say our father,
while staring at her toes.
Everyone had answers
I could not understand
so braced by pipe and bottle,
took an existential stand.

Blind Prisoners

Life passing distorted,
through jaded eyes,
watching every wrong,
weighing every right,
seldom listening,
always fighting,
never hearing,
blindly seeing,
embracing visions of what cannot be,
leaping minor hedges,
peering through fences,
but never breaching the barracoon.

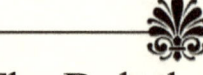
The Deluded Hipster

Those paranoid flashes and boxcar blues,
casting about for something to do.
Man in a suit will lend us shoes.
Can't run away. No reason to stay.
They'd never fit us anyway.

He says the time has come;
but don't want something new.
Must go on but it's all undone;
so score a lid and away we run.
Those paranoid flashes and boxcar blues.

Bus Station Blues

Beat, close, decrepit bus station,
guardian of a winter night's fears,
tenuous refuge from darkness.
Wait, walk, and wander;
prowling through its guts
and sterile, cigarette-butt embrace.

Sharing the Ride

Pacing the bus station's tile floor,
on winter's cold snowless night,
waiting for a bus delayed,
unsure his choice was right.
Watched him standing by;
a stray waif and melancholy sight,

The silver-gray bus arrives,
sweating oil, heat, and diesel.
He wobbles up aluminum stairs,
searching out a window
for woven polyester sleep;
then, waiting impatiently to leave,
watches the tourist slide in beside.

Passing Bus Windows

Climbing roads twist through villages,
between stark, gray, granite churches,
past verdigris copper spires,
decaying from weather, age, and pride.
Black patches scar snow-blanketed ground;
homes with fading crests and barns with hexes,
their clapboard skin weathered chalk-white.
Skeletal winter hardwoods,
stand bare against swaying pines,
as nature prevails with time.

North Camp Twilight

North Camp boomed as virgin forests fell,
then vanished with endless green tracts,
leaving a blanched, buckling sawmill;
machinery gone, beams exposed, rafters collapsing;
surrounded by dull, shrunken sawdust piles;
weed-streaked on the malnourished grass.
Across the blacktop; human stragglers
struggle to make their stand
between faded white village signs
at the mountain crossroads
in a flat clearing near the river.

Lackluster log roadhouse; gas station and store
on the two-lane asphalt highway
collecting gravel roads from second-growth forests.
High country gateway, estranged from the world,
sustained by travelers and diminishing hunters;
until deep winter's frozen isolation shrouds all with snow.

Below the trees, in brush and meadows
sheltering whitetails, bears, fox, and birds;
a blossoming of abandoned outbuildings
behind weathered, glass-crowned gas pumps.
Fading wood, peeling paint, doors ajar, broken panes;
walls partly sheathed by cracked, black tarpaper.
Alongside the abandoned narrow-gauge roadbed,
once alive with steam-sweated Shay engines
dragging cars of rough-sawn wood, machinery, and supplies.
Now a broken, decaying trail of creosoted ties;
their steel rails long since scavenged from
an easy grade marked by bent spikes,
rusted tie plates, and scattered stone ballast.

Outback are shacks and minor buildings
in a field overrun with brush, poplars,
and eighty-seven years of cast-offs.
Survival's detritus surround the disused outhouse,
derelict sheds, and defunct logging wheel.
Faded green Studebaker pickup with large, bullet cowl lights;
rust-brown Diamond Reo wrecker with muscular safety-rims;
black Hupmobile, hoodless with dry-rotted water hoses;
Volkswagen split-window Beetle absent glass or wheels;
played out, faded-green John Deere G;
two small, gray Fordson tractors;
red De Soto Adventurer wedged between saplings;
and black Model A sedan with steel top replacement.
Steel carcasses all; slowly weathering away.

Inside the pedestrian, log roadhouse,
behind paneled timbers;
three hunters from a tent camp
attended by an ageless woman;
thick-waisted, beat, and
puffing a glowing cigarette;
its white filter stained by red lipstick.
Nearby, a ponderous mate
and composite son.

The tourist orders a grilled hamburger,
pressing for directions as it sputters.
Greasy patty on plain, soggy bun
with tasteless, pale yellow beer.
Shuffling out to pump gas
for sparse, restless customers
their son looks into a moonless black universe;
deep, endless, and bristling with stars.
Each breath mists in the still night's chill.
Only plows and snowmobiles
will make North Camp come winter;
but he'll follow the tourist west long before.

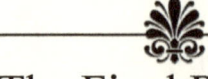

The Final Redoubt

Only the large fieldstone farmhouse survives;
a rustic steakhouse under August's sun
surrounded by asphalt parking lots,
streets, sidewalks, stores, and auto dealership.

The bucolic, white barn; gone.
Hayloft, stable, and milk-house; gone.
Tall brown-tile silos, pigpen, chicken coop; gone.
Lane between spreading trees and bushes, gone.
Twittering birds and whizzing grasshoppers, gone.
Fallow, plowed, and planted fields; gone.
Rock-piles, orchard, woodlot, and white bee hives; gone.

A quarter-section farm, carved from the land
by sweating horses, family, and hired men.
A child's walk to their one-room school.
A home on the trail to village church, gristmill,
bank, hardware, and general store.
A weekly excursion by foot, horse, carriage,
pickup, then family car.

Children left for town and city,
the trail graveled then paved,
the first gray Fordson tractor coughed in,
the draft horses and harnesses sold off,
the electricity began flowing between creosoted poles,
the outhouse left to wasps and spiders,
the brick smokehouse unused.

Its woven wire fencerow along the lane
between fertile fields to the back forty
long since rusted, rotted, and vanished.

Woodlot and orchard trees forgotten.
The bouquet of alfalfa's light blue flowers,
saturated manure, and fresh-cut corn stalks
exchanged for rotting garbage, cooking grease,
exhaust, black tar, and bleached concrete;
all baking in summer-heated stillness.

A solitary green fragment remains;
isolated from its stone farmhouse
by cement block buildings and parking lots,
blacktop marked by fading white lines,
and scuffed concrete wheel stops.
The small refuge, alienated and unsound;
shrunk, bounded, and trapped
by cracked and broken asphalt
constrained with gray-white curbs.
The surviving alfalfa patch;
a living residue, unused, untended, and unnoticed;
a bountiful field's last redoubt;
between McDonald's and the lively fuel plaza
encircled by surplus commercial lots.

Descendants of long-dead or devoured
crickets, ants, and grasshoppers
chirp and whirr amidst knee-high weeds,
scattered alfalfa clumps, and wildflowers.
Insects and snakes share this sanctuary
below small birds nesting in leaves and stalks;
adjacent to short, manicured grass lawns.

For an instant, a moment, an afternoon,
those passing by glimpse what was lost;
the final fragment, reduced and besieged by traffic,
marking time until its trifling apocalypse.

A Spectral Haven

Meandering river to the bay,
running broad and shallow,
severed from a dead channel
with narrow mouth silted solid;
stranding a deserted port and harbor;
condemning them to stagnation
and fomenting sodden desolation.

High ground brush and hardwood
digesting the abandoned, packed-dirt road;
further isolating this decaying haven.
Uncertain shoreline, irregular and indistinct,
encircles barren tree trunks stripped of bark;
their dull white skeletons streaked with gray.

Blanched piers, wharfs, slips, and docks;
embraced by stranded hulls, masts, and spars;
their wood indistinguishable from expired trees.
Bark, brig, schooner, barge, yacht, and tug
settling below the dark, unmoving water,
alongside launch, cutter, and pinnace.

Some resisting oblivion retain a past form.
One ragged steel funnel cants slightly;
a rusting, red-brown, blackened tombstone
in this bleak palette spread across shimmering, crystal-black water.
Gunnels awash, cul-de-sac companionways,
rotting sheathing, bare frames, and collapsing bulkheads.
Splintered hatch covers rise from decaying decks.
Resilient standing rigging, slack and blackening;
orange-tinged wire rope stripped of parceling.
Rusting chains, buckler plates, capstans, and cleats.

Transparent surface water's tranquil ebony
overlays thick green-black algae blooms,
obscuring the bottom and brushing its surface;
their softly clinging, scratching dark shapes
haphazardly pierced and pinioned
by fractured spars and shattered mast trunks
rising from purgatory's warm, languid embrace.

Piers and docks separating from a mud shore;
retreating from derelict, decomposing buildings;
skeletal cadavers encircling this silent, brooding crypt
beyond a collapsing wharf caught in repose
as persistent grass reclaims compacted ground.

Stagnant water caresses shore, pilings, and hulls;
devoid of frogs, fish, turtles, or water spiders;
silent, still, and close under insipid gray skies
devoid of dragon flies, black flies, and mosquitoes;
absent birds gliding overhead to leave droppings.

Disowned by the river, forsaken by humanity,
left quiescent to the surreal, sterile swamp
steadily consuming prostrate husks;
where time worries derelicts and relics,
silently embracing inescapable extinction.

Interstate Night

Concrete lanes slip silently below a curving hood;
the strobing centerline lit by diverted low-beams,
then fading silently away in silvered mirrors.
Mile-marker 50 ghosting past, glowing green;
luminous instruments gleaming in the dark night,
rearview mirror truck lights growing bright,
a blinding flash then sudden passing shape,
red taillights shrink into the vanishing point;
a solitary universe moving, moving, moving.

Concrete lanes slip silently below a curving hood;
the strobing centerline lit by diverted low-beams,
then fading silently away in silvered mirrors.
Mile-marker 75 ghosting past, glowing green;
just beyond sloping, curving concrete ramps
flanking another isolated double overpass;
its travel plaza blazing under artificial sunlight;
a solitary universe moving, moving, moving.

Concrete lanes slip silently below a curving hood;
the strobing centerline lit by diverted low-beams,
then fading silently away in silvered mirrors.
Mile-marker 100 ghosting past, glowing green;
darkness cloaking a mysterious sleeping world
past the shoulder, beyond the light, below the stars;
dark ghostly shapes sliding silently by;
trees, fields, barns, homes, billboards, streams.
Endless fenced lives flowing steadily past;
a solitary universe moving, moving, moving.

Concrete lanes slip silently below a curving hood;
the strobing centerline lit by diverted low-beams,

then fading silently away in silvered mirrors.
Mile-marker 125 ghosting past, glowing green;
window cracked, a fecund countryside night,
humming rubber, blaring radio, sipping coffee;
a solitary universe moving, moving, moving.

Concrete lanes slip silently below a curving hood;
the strobing centerline lit by diverted low-beams,
then fading silently away in silvered mirrors.
Mile-marker 160 ghosting past, glowing green;
in the lush, pregnant riparian night,
flashing over a broad waterway,
the great, captive mother-river
flowing south past New Orleans to the Gulf.
Tires roll jubilantly over the painted state line,
a solitary universe cruising through darkness,
driving west across America;
the high plains by morning and Denver by midnight.

North to Boulder

Three like souls struggle to stay awake,
gliding through Arizona's desolate night,
their tank is full and wine bottle half.
The radio blares, stations change,
trucks ghost pass provincial sage,
transient moments fade;
and tomorrow, Boulder.

The Hill Mythology

Frayed, twisting asphalt snaking down Boulder Canyon
towards rolling foothills, cushioning Colorado's high plains
from the Rockies' green slopes and chameleonic Flatirons
below barren gray-granite peaks' melting snowcaps.

Constricted, guided, controlled, and framed
by rust-streaked hard-rock faces;
sweating cold water into the racing, rock-strewn riverbed;
along a road supplanting tracks, trails, and paths
of Indians, mountain men, and prospectors.
Trucks, cars, and motorcycles now climb,
or compression-brake down, through the canyon
where Ute families lived, loved, and bathed.
Overrun by wealthy Northeast progeny
wearing tribal dress, ragged work clothes, or nothing;
to passively taunt harvesting police cruisers.

Spreading beyond the canyon mouth;
light-tan high plains stretch east
to the far, bending horizon.
Scattered, shimmering reservoirs;
mirrors scattered below blue, cloudless skies;
an infinite checkerboard of farms
spread over boundless flatland.

Surging between Boulder Canyon's stone walls,
coming from primeval mountains and fertile parks;
the twisting stream rushing vibrant and cold
divides branches, splits, and splinters to muddy trickles
irrigating uncounted rows of green barley shoots.

Hot, tacky blacktop broadens near its mouth,

shearing into divided concrete lanes
sharing their manicured grass median.
A boulevard for tourists and privileged iconoclasts;
leaving top-drawer stereos in canyon shacks
to drive Mustangs, Jaguars, Camaros, Cadillacs,
Morgans, Porsche roadsters, plebeian beetles,
and one ornamental microbus.

A still-born steel building skeleton
rises to one side; waiting to be razed
for a more modern, larger jailhouse;
replacing one forever overbooked
with transients, accused, and convicted.
Two concrete lanes bloom to five,
with smooth curbs severed by passing side streets
where overhanging trees curtain old buildings;
chalking white, in resigned anticipation
of demolition, renting, or renewal.

Overhead traffic signal on a wire,
flashing yellow by the county building.
Turn onto a gentle climb to The Hill,
past mundane residential side streets
then another turn and just a little further.

The Hill arises, suddenly without notice;
another world: transitory, chimerical, animated.
Its red-brick storefronts resisting glass and steel.
A Boulder neighborhood loathed by locals;
one haunted by transients, various freaks, and students.
Scholars, poets, communists, anarchists, and neo-hippies
crashing or living where they land; for as long as they can.
A minuscule, tawdry portrayal of their mythical Paris;
and avant-garde underground until metamorphous,
expels eccentrics, bankers, lawyers, and bishops.

An inescapable human bouquet,
permeates streets, sidewalks, alleys,
head shops, bookstores, and bars.

Beat wood houses from the vanished century
loom above this vibrant, noisy crossroads.
Garbage, carbon monoxide, and police substation narcs
mix with marijuana's burnt alfalfa scent wafting past.

The Sink stands proud on its corner;
two large rooms in a brick building,
graffiti-covered basement walls.
Long-haired, slightly-stoned freaks,
serving lukewarm, golden Coors on tap.
Restless travelers and leather-jacketed men
eye unharnessed women in patched jeans;
seeking and demanding without compromise.

Tulagi's hawking a new rock band,
exuding much greater class,
extracting a cover charge.
Light or dark Coors in one great room,
two rows of church-hard wood benches,
face the raised musicians' dais.
Parishioners drink sullenly, steadily;
deep in conversation, unless the band is good
or someone rises to shake, dance, and sing.

The Hill thrusts and writhes nightly
beneath small, glowing electric suns.
Lounge, loiter, and deal near its crossroad,
and along the teeming main street.
Honest vagrants collide with students in mufti,
spare change artists seeking an easy touch,
dirty people in patched, faded blue-jeans,
perfumed people wearing leather patches,
and minnow-elites strutting in leather shirts and trousers;
mostly affluent masquerading as proletariat.

Corner cafe, hand-painted sign
trumpeting world's best hamburgers.
King of the Hill Record shop
squeezes a waiting pawnbroker,

against the ice cream parlor;
near a clothing store window
where high-laced ankle boots
look out on the curbed Morgan roadster.
A battered red Bonneville coughs past,
weaving aggressively through heavy traffic.

People walking along the sidewalks;
cruising, searching, existing, or waiting.
Some mumble harshly, "Buy-a-lid"
despite the prowling narcs.
A brazen red-haired freak,
stringy, unkempt, and pungent,
seeking cash buyers, steps forward grinning,
shoots out his clenched hand, "Mescallini?"
Spring's gentle evening air caresses,
a squatting panhandler with heavy breasts
earnestly reaching out to those most likely.
Honking cars converse; quick, long, or angry.
Breathe deep, mile high air is thin.

Yellow Buick Wildcat convertible, top down,
glides impervious through milling crowds,
over the crosswalk, ignoring a pink light,
then coasts off The Hill for Denver.
A black knucklehead motorcycle passes,
extended chrome forks thrust forward;
conveying a head in dirty leathers sans colors.
Freaks gather outside Five Flags restaurant,
joking, smoking, toking, laughing, and shoving;
briefly split by a footsore transient striding past,
up the sidewalk's concrete with bulging backpack
topped by rolled foam-rubber pad.

Loitering in its warm pungent night,
paired beat cops walk, observe, stop, question.
Freshly pressed, short-sleeved blue uniforms.
Black patent leather holsters reflecting streetlight
hang heavy with semiautomatic pistols.

Varnished nightsticks for tonight;
conserving their long, bare cudgels for spring,
when the tear-gas spewing, armored fury flies;
but tonight its rotor's clipped and Boulder quiet.
Shift's ending, no need dragging it out.
Tulagi's first; for police no cover.
A long respite taken when Kershaw plays;
far less if street action erupts.

Looming above The Hill's unequal roofs,
towering Flatirons are turning black,
dark, and foreboding in fading light.
Tombstone slabs jammed against mountains,
below bright stars and faint cotton cloud wisps.
Headlights flow along mountain roads like blazing arteries,
snaking and slithering against dark, distance mounds;
following the old trails through brisk, high mountain passes;
then Central City, Georgetown, and Glenwood Springs.

Another Colorado summer evening turns to night,
transformed to early morning as stragglers drift off
towards dorms, homes, rooms, or bolt-holes.
The Hill empties then lays quiet under streetlights;
passing time until dawn foretells another rendezvous;
of ephemeral time and circumstance
where yesterday, today, and tomorrow collide
then inexorably fade to memory and myth.

Aficionado

Overlooking The Hill's crossroad
in a rented second-floor room,
thick with smoldering incense
impregnating furniture
creating a personal aura
beneath kaleidoscope posters;
he reclines in a thrift-store couch,
vibrating gently to the stereo's throbbing base.
Shades drawn, room gently lit,
glowing blue fluorescent black light,
for atmosphere and quartering acid.

Sparse beard, thinning blond hair,
patched jeans and Mexican wedding shirt.
Sorting seeds and stems in a board game cover,
ecstatic to discover grass cut with opium;
muddy black, grape-scented carbuncles.

Cursing fickle Western Slope friends
who refused to score horse tranquilizer
so he must harvest and dry his children;
tall, green plants climbing a kite-string trellis,
thriving under artificial light
behind folding closet doors.

Speeding through final examinations,
then home across the great plains;
a two-cycle dull-red Saab cruising through
farmland, town, and city to the coast.

Next year he joins his father's firm
donning white shirt, blue suit, and tie;

trading, selling, buying in office and pit,
marrying another trust-fund scion,
finishing off each day with three martinis,
raising two beau monde children,
sending them west to downhill ski,
and study no more than necessary;
renewing the privileged cycle
of a class without consequence.

A Gentle Innocent

Buster lives near the university. His large snow-white beard shows gray roots and each day he chooses between mangled ball caps or a tall, blue antique police helmet. In his late thirties, forties, or fifties; no one knows. He claims past years are irrelevant so they're ignored; disavowal being the antidote for whatever. At his thrift shop haberdashery he pays cash in crumpled green bills extracted from a shirt pocket. His résumé boasts six weeks Navy, two months disc jockey, one afternoon pumping gas, and more. The unpublished philosopher slips into lecture classes' rear seats and often intervenes with couples suffering unwilling or infertile husbands. He regularly confers with Barney who is God, or God who is Barney, but no matter since he and Barney embrace every faith.

Today Buster's sipping herbal tea and dunking molasses cookies in the same student union where a week before he announced his approaching nuptials. A rotund widow and country club bar patron who has claimed to be thirty-nine for decades must replace a beloved tomcat; and Buster believes he will do well in society.

Getting Right

Ignore untreatable wounds,
ignore oppression,
ignore suppression,
ignore lunacy,
ignore subjugation,
ignore responsibility,
ignore accountability;
be impervious.

Embrace ignorance,
embrace class,
embrace race,
embrace barriers,
embrace ideology,
embrace religion,
embrace academia,
embrace good war,
embrace silence;
be rewarded,
but never forgiven.

Rites of Spring '72

Young men and boys know;
their lottery numbers,
the distant foreign war,
its unpronounceable places,
thousands dead, wounded, and crippled,
justifications shifting weekly,
with tissue paper rationalizations.
One failed course ends deferment
for those shielded by the university;
for those not enrolled it's Canada, jail, or go;
unless someone at the country club,
speaks with the man who makes things right.

Low and slow bombers mined Haiphong;
revealed to the nation during a spring night.
Hearsay roils Boulder's capricious campus.
Talk, phones, radios, and television screens
flash like summer heat lightening
across academia's mountain citadel.
Fatigue, frustration, impotence;
rage under a cloudless blue sky,
within tan sandstone buildings
beneath red tile roofs.
Polemic activists harangue the students
moving between dorm, class, and union;
leading dogs, lusting, studying, or leaving.
Grass and revolution disrupt and thicken thin foothill air.
Boulder's spring ritual and rite of passage ignites.

Radical cadres gather; finding opportunity in rarified air.
Passionate speakers blossom along sidewalks.
Revolution blooms from cerebral fertilizer,

composted from every voguish cause;
distant from the twenty-eighth street overpass
where a dozen students squat on hot pavement,
gaining another dozen and watched by uncommitted curious.
Traffic slows, halts, then grudgingly reroutes;
spontaneous reaction without direction.
Too early for elite student leaders' white bullhorns,
but they loiter near the student union,
safeguarding future aspirations.

On campus, safely distant, well clear, radical cadres harangue;
as grass and revolution disrupt then thicken thin foothill air.

Forming across broad, grayish concrete,
blue uniforms with long unvarnished batons prepare;
and police advance,
with one small group probing forward.
Butts burning on hot, rough concrete,
scared, defiant, afraid to break;
and police advance.
Stand, back off, or melt away;
sweating comrades remain,
exuding agitated fear;
and police advance.
Those who'll stand link hands,
butts burning on hot, rough concrete,
unforgiving in the morning sun
overpowering a gentle mountain breeze;
and police advance.

A hundred uniforms approach in formation,
halt on command, fit goggle-eyed masks.
"Teargas in three-minutes; teargas in three-minutes."
The peace chant gaining volume and cohesion,
disrupted by "Fuck you" or "Join us";
and police advance.
Word passes; be ready to take gas,
some seasoned speak to uneasy initiates,
some abscond,

some anticipate later dope, parties, and sex.
some seek sanctuary across the street,
some see their future at risk;
and police advance.

On campus, safely distant, well clear, radical cadres harangue;
as grass and revolution disrupt then thicken thin foothill air.

The peace chant volume grows,
heartening the few remaining resisters,
taken up by those gathering in the wings;
and police advance.
Most plan to sprint when tear gas arcs in.
The fish chant follows.
One student in the dwindling redoubt,
standing firm on hot, rough concrete,
rises above sitting comrades,
points at the closing solid blue lines,
"You, third from the left, you're out of step!"
And police advance.

The blue formation keeps coming, silent and steady,
white helmets with dark face-shields down,
three-foot unvarnished batons across chests,
through the overpass towards these squatters;
and police advance.

The knot stands firm, arms-locked and scared;
wanting to run, hearing unintelligible commands.
A single, blue-gray gas grenade,
pin pulled, spewing choking white clouds,
spins across the hot concrete pavement.
The small redoubt erupts and runs, eyes burning.
Bullet-like projectiles spin forward, arcing to either side;
and police advance.
Veterans mark the breeze,
step upwind as white clouds drift past.
Tenderfeet run, rest, run, walk, run;
over galvanized steel guardrails, across freshly mown grass,

colliding with those indifferent, those unaffected;
walking to class along asphalt trails.

On campus, safely distant, well clear, radical cadres harangue;
as grass and revolution disrupt then thicken thin foothill air.

Protestors, resisters, students, bystanders cheer,
pull shirts over faces, return to the pavement;
reform beyond still-smoking canisters
spreading white clouds through campus.
Planes circle overhead, looking down, running cameras.
A tenuous pause; derisions hurled at silent police;
charred tear gas canisters of blue steel burn hands raw;
and police stand.
"Ambulance coming through, make a path;
ambulance coming through, make a path."
A white van rolls slowly though the unsettled front.
Towards police? Who knows? Another follows.
Who's hurt? No one knows but milling crowds part.

Motorcycles weave through,
making good their agile escape.
More tear gas arcs into the crowd;
a police car rolls down the road,
pulsing white smoke through an open window.
People jump aside as it disappears
and some search for rocks.
"No violence, no violence, no violence."
A garbage truck passes through;
the stalemate holds;
and police advance,
and police halt,
and police reform,
and the crowd regroups;
then advance, halt, retreat, return.

Americans want a fair-fight.
This is foreign, frustrating, infuriating.
Anti-warriors struggling not to;

stomachs sick, eyes burning,
finding nonviolence hard, oppressive.
No strategy, no leadership,
strength through weakness;
an impenetrable jelly resistance,
resiliency from open space behind;
and police advance,
and police halt,
and police reform,
and the crowd regroups;
then advance, halt, retreat, return.

On campus, safely distant, well clear, radical cadres harangue;
as grass and revolution disrupt then thicken thin foothill air.

A disoriented lady's warned away,
a mother jogs to her gray Datsun
two babes in tow; all helped along.
Non-violence holds tough
as support increases.
The growing swarm braces for gas,
challenging, clapping, yelling
beneath a sky threatening rain;
existing, standing, holding on.

Stones thrown, canisters soar,
as adversaries face off;
and police advance.
A smoking tear gas round
strikes the Lazy J Motel roof,
beside a ventilation intake,
disgorging guests onto the street.
Families and businessmen,
weave unmolested through protestors.
The swarm scatters then coheres, filling the street,
welcoming pails of water that arrive,
far too little for flushing eyes;
enough to spread gas residue
and worsen the burn.

Spectators watch; some cheer.
A white Nova bulls through,
unstoppable, its horn blasting;
drowning admonitions,
"No rocks, no rocks, no rocks!"
And police advance,
and police halt,
and police reform,
and the crowd regroups;
advance, halt, retreat, advance.

On campus, safely distant, well clear, radical cadres harangue;
as grass and revolution disrupt then thicken thin foothill air.

Police demand an incongruous rush hour truce;
not accepted, Nixon cursed, epithets loosed.
Burned hands, skin, and eyes.
Fatigue, frustration, and impotence
pulse under clouding, darkening heavens.
Another large crowd gathers
back at the twenty-eighth street overpass;
and police retreat.

Spinning gas canisters arc overhead,
or rocket through the crowd,
waist-high before crashing against cement curbs
to spiral skyward trailing white plumes;
or twirl across pavement spewing gas;
and police advance,
waving long, unvarnished truncheons,
sending strike groups from their formation,
swinging hard to smash all within arm's length,
sweeping up the slow, stunned, and stupid.
Flocking spectators flee, scatter, regroup;
and police retreat to the overpass,
shielding townspeople from confrontation.

Rumors, rumors, and more rumors;
people gathering at Broadway and Pearl,

the student union has been gassed.
An ambulance passes.
A round skids over another flat roof
and Skyland Motel guests flee.
A family crosses the double highway;
ignored as they debate anti-warriors.

On campus, safely distant, well clear, radical cadres harangue;
as grass and revolution disrupt then thicken thin foothill air.

The rain comes, then slowly builds,
flushing tear gas into burning eyes.
People stare into a graying sky,
prop eyelids open to the rain.
Cars gunning loudly, trying to ram through,
are stopped, surrounded, released;
and police advance,
and police halt,
and police reform,
and the crowd regroups;
then advance, halt, retreat, return.

More rain, heavier rain, fewer people;
more rain, heavier rain, fewer police;
then steady rain washes conflict away;
police depart; most protestors follow.
The mountain air grows fresh,
the warm spring evening begins.
Anti-warriors recover;
regrouping across Boulder,
preparing for the night.
Tet is three years past, Haiphong is mined.

On campus, safely distant, well clear, radical cadres harangue;
as grass and revolution disrupt then thicken thin foothill air;
potpourri demands compiled, white bullhorns readied,
and their relentless corrosion begins without risk.

Transient Tolerance

Evening's thick-lipped sage,
mused no hate was right,
that intellectuals knew no race;
Then came the night.

Perpetual Resistance

Righteous fists thrown high;
strike off tyrants' chains;
then cursing shouts
from those just freed,
leave none to fight,
but you and me.

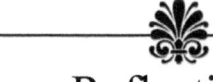

Reflections

The unseeing,
the opponents,
the unbelievers,
the hesitant,
the questioners'
bones were broken,
bodies trampled for the cause;
until all righteousness
was perfectly fouled.

Redux in Black

Organize, anti-fascists, organize;
black boots, black helmets,
black face shields, clubs, bear spray.
Resist, silence, intimidate, coerce.

Organize, anti-fascists, organize;
darting disruptive schools of hate;
feeding off others, devoured by their own.
No action, thought, word, or fact escapes.
Speech, freedom, and civility
bow to intolerance, ignorance, and hate.

Organize, anti-fascists, organize;
crush fascists, conservatives,
moderates, liberals, and doubters.
Never let them inflict mutated logic
on their righteous, or the dull masses.
Any measure, any hurt, any injustice
necessary for the cause; to hold the line.

Present is past donning a new color;
and the future?

Forty Acres and a Mule

The poet's life companion;
long, thin nose over scraggy beard,
following the balding Beat
with stringy white mane;
cajoling his ardent herd.

The poet guru's life companion,
says school's no place to learn,
better to make your stand,
with forty acres, a mule;
live off the fat of our land.

Western Exile

Looking to the mountains reveals little
while longing for Northern Michigan's beauty;
wasted on those who cannot see
beyond blowing snow, naked shivering trees
through barren months preceding spring.
The West's a painting but East is home,
with friends who must care but seldom write.
Abandoned in Boulder, hungry, isolated, and alone.

Sangre de Cristo

Evening's red sun sinks through thin air, vanishing behind southern Colorado Rockies' snow-topped peaks. The approaching night's chill blankets wet granite outcroppings alongside a blacktop highway blasted through high mountains. One dark bird crosses the still-warm road, glides over a gently murmuring stream and thinly grassed slope to an anorexic bush surviving in lean topsoil.

A tourist walked this road towards the divide, keeping to its inside shoulder, turning when he heard a car, raising his thumb, then dropping it as they climb past. One golden ride whisked him across the mother river and high plains to Boulder; then another due south to Pueblo. His last score took him past Canyon City prison, Salida, and Poncha Springs before fortune turned and spirit waned.

He now walks slowly; every movement rote. Faded blue jeans mottled with assorted cloth and leather patches match his jacket with long white streaks. It mostly covers a chambray shirt; long-sleeved and worn thin. Supple Red Wing work-boots fit comfortably except thinning soles ensure tender feet feel the hot, sticky surface as he advances; one foot then the other. His green duffle discarded as too bulky and its single strap ungainly; leaving him the army surplus canvas rucksack. A low-crowned, wide-brimmed brown felt hat perches on stringy sun-streaked hair falling below his shoulders. The sun-burnt face is framed by a thin, almost pubescent beard.

A car's low hum raises hope but the Buick thrusts its chrome nose around a granite outcropping then spurns his extended arm with a soft rush of air. The couple arguing in its front seat takes no notice but their offspring make faces in the rear window as it climbs towards the crest. Resigned to a mountain night, he checks the road, leaves its narrow gravel shoulder, feels the stillness, crosses over, and threads through clinging brush to a grassy embankment alongside the burbling stream.

This tourist settles on a small green extension into flowing water where grass is thicker and he'll be out of sight. Trying to ignore an aching back, sore arms, tender feet, and painful shoulders, he slowly chews the last peanuts from a bag that sustained him since leaving the flatland. Concerned an overnight downpour could flood this small sanctuary the exhausted traveler briefly considers moving before sliding into a faded red, goose-down sleeping bag bought secondhand; smelling of past occupants and their campfires. His tired body warms the sack as he sleeps fitfully under a clear, starless mountain sky; half-waking when eighteen-wheelers climbing the steep grade downshift or compression brake while coasting. He intermittently shifts position to fit the ground until awakened by voices of men stopping to paint wet designs on the shoulder. They're ignored and he falls asleep for another hour before waking to a cool, clear mountain morning.

His sleeping bag's nylon skin is damp from dew but he rolls it up, packs, and resumes the pilgrimage. Yesterday's inauspicious karma proves unshakeable. Every car whether old, new, full or empty slides cautiously past and large trucks cannot pause on that grade. His stomach tightens and thirst grows while the sun rises sufficiently to heat this lofty canyon.

Salvation slows and jerks to a stop. An arm beckons from its open window behind flowing fenders under fading blue paint. A small Chevrolet stake truck with rear duals gasping up and west stops long enough for its driver to shove the passenger door open. Built of thick American steel the year this tourist was born, one door mirror's missing, tires bald, and interior scented by sawdust, pastures, irrigation, and cattle.

The good samaritan is swarthy and powerfully compact with muscular, sun-reddened arms thrusting from a simple western work-shirt with faux-pearl snap-buttons. Some gray is visible in short, black hair spilling from the brim of a red, sweat-stained COOP ball-cap. Crisp blue jeans conceal two pointed-toed cowboy boots' upper leather. His savior's grin seems permanently fixed to a beard-stubble face and there's the faint, lingering smell of a morning bath using scented soap mixing with mint dipping tobacco.

Clutch, shift, and gas instantly bring his truck to life as the welcoming door slams shut. The driver leans forward into the hill, urging his chariot upward, taking curves in short chords, and talking nonstop.

"Where, ya from?"

"Iron Mountain."
"Where's that?"
"Michigan."
"Hear you've got big barns back east."
"They're further south."
"What brings you out here?"
"Something different."
"Find it?"
"Not yet."
"Hungary?"
"Yes."
"Bet that's different."

Their ascent with curves, ditches, and hundred-foot drops is exhilarating but surpassed by the descent; careening off the mountains' backbone only slightly restrained by the transmission's worn gears and smoldering brake shoes. Rock walls and boulders flash past with wind from open windows clawing at the tourist's hat until he removes it.

They nearly bypass the small mountain gas station wedged in a wide spot along the road that likely disappears under winter snow. The blue truck half-slides as it skids through dusty gravel before crunching to a halt before the single red gas pump with obsolete glass crown. Beef jerky and molasses cookie packages leer at the tourist from their window display as gas gurgling into a tank behind the seat is heard and smelt.

The launch varies little from their landing then his benefactor continues speaking while shifting, swerving, and slowing where rocks encroach on the lane, "Always wanted to travel, see things. A lot of guys work up at the dam or in the oilfields. Pay's good but I prefer cattle and carpentry. Irrigate when there's nothing else but that's hard on the back. Got married out of high school. Everyone did then; except them that was drafted. She's a good woman. Little more meat on her now but holding up after our children. We'll get a pickup camper and travel when they're off." The tourist began nodding off against the steel doorframe until brought back by a jovial, "Don't fall asleep and miss the cafe."

At the second roadside leveling, broader than the first, a miniature park accommodated the small mountain restaurant converted from a house. This agreeable refuge extended several hundred feet behind to the rock cliff-face. A fast, shiny, cold mountain stream split the miniature park with crystal water submerging, circumventing, and colliding over a rock-strewn bed. The building's one-time front yard had become a broad swath of dusty pea-stone gravel packed with cars, pickups with rifle racks, and an empty Peterbuilt tractor-trailer logging truck.

Beyond an aluminum door, the white clapboard house's two front rooms were combined to create its dining area; and beside the entrance door a counter containing ornate cash register, toothpick dispenser, and steel spike impaling green cash slips. The diminutive jukebox jammed in one corner emitted a melodic, silky voice wailing over true love lost to a rival competes with chatter over linoleum-topped, tightly packed, steel tables. Two women hustle back and forth through swinging doors to the compact kitchen; serving food, circulating among patrons, and clearing tables. Each time these louvered half-doors swing the tourist catches another glimpse inside.

His savior orders two roast beef sandwiches, mashed potatoes, and thick brown gravy before leaning forward, "It's good food and we're in luck; often as not you wait for a table. Today's on me since I take a different road home and won't leave you hungry." He smiled, sat back against the chair's vinyl back, took in the chatter, and briefly closed his eyes.

Sustenance and bliss came on faded white ceramic plates with their blue trim worn near away and clean silverware equally fatigued; but hot, filling, and heaven-sent. A grateful tourist ate while people paid and left, entered then worked through to an open spot, or gossiped with others waiting. Locals patiently endured while travelers slipped nervously back through the door. The tourist's patron jousted with their hostess while at the cash register; displaying familiarity and affection. Bright sunlight waiting outside reflected from their truck's blue paint like a dull jewel. Its driver extracted a mangled toothpick, grinning as he pulled the door open, "Katharine's a saint."

The truck came instantly to life and launched from the graveled lot in a dust cloud that hung unmoving several seconds then drifted across the blacktop to a slope seeded with small boulders. The descent resumed for five miles much as before except the tourist's stomach was full and he enjoyed more peace than he could remember. This continued with him slouching in the cracked leather seat until his savior slowed then halted just before a narrow road climbing the mountain through dense lodgepole pines. Grinning, he nodded towards it, "My father's mansions are up there. You'll soon have a ride but watch out for the patrol on the flatlands. They work hitchhikers and out-of-state plates during summers but the sheriff's one of us so he might just put you up in jail for the night."

With a last wave he threw the truck in gear and began climbing the narrow track with its shear drop, potholes, washouts, tight turns, and uneven stretches. It seemed passable for a short distance then little more than fading path. The tourist watched him vanish around its first bend then began walking. Downhill was easier, the highway warm, mountain air thin, and quiet punctuated only by chirping insects. A white bird flew overhead, circled, and left. The tourist tracked it to vanishing then an unremarkable sedan appeared; coasting down black asphalt. His hand shot out, thumb extended. The driver slowed then eased over, not quite half off the roadway, and motioned to its rear door. An elated tourist pulled it open, gently set his rucksack on cloth seat covers, and slid in behind the bench seat. Its nondescript, decorous driver seemed more welcoming than his wife, but both pleasant. Smiling as they eased cautiously back onto the road, his new benefactor says, "I'm Father Samuel this is my wife Anna. We're traveling to our new congregation in Delta. You seemed lost out here by yourself."

"Yes, a local man picked me up the other side of the divide. We had lunch at a cafe six miles back but he lives somewhere on the mountain and just turned off."

The woman looked puzzled, "We picked up snacks at a gas station to tide us over but never saw a cafe; and he can't live far up that road. Our map says it's impassable and there's a note warning it went to an old abandoned mining town several miles further up the mountain that washed away years ago."

Swan Song

A thousand mountain acres above Telluride
following the broad meandering valley;
reawakening beneath a snow comforter
retreating up greening aspen slopes.
Lofty stone peaks; white and granite against a clear sky,
towering over thinly grassed parks and meadows,
shedding spring's cold water in countless rivulets,
shrinking resilient gray-white snow redoubts,
flowing down slopes, valleys, and rivers
to delight children swimming flatland irrigation ditches.

Crisp high country air with lodgepole pine's piquant scent.
Sparse growth awakened by the spring sun's grudging warmth;
melding earth and air under limitless skies daubed with wisp-clouds.
A zephyr breeze flows over its solitary grease-mud road
winding up from Ridgeway between mountain pastures,
splitting the damp, awakening valley,
curving past one living ranch among the deserted,
then plummeting down through a narrow canyon
to the black asphalt road for Telluride.

Off a sedate curve along this dirt track
in quiet slumber behind weathered pole fencing;
a small ranch abandoned over winter comes alive.
Frame house, two-stories, wood shingles, mostly empty;
stained double mattress, rusty springs, and dull brass bed.
Dust-clouded rear panes half-light its neglected parlor
looking up the sloping irrigated horse pasture
with winter's debris chaotically diverting water.

Beyond a frame door, rusty screen, and sash spring,
the barn stands with broken glass and empty hayloft.

Backed up to the rough-wood loading chute
opening on the lodgepole pine corral,
a tired Chevrolet flat-rack with weak springs
disgorges summer heifers, steers, and cows,
as faded white racks convulse to bellies and hooves;
summer cattle shortly released to meadows
rapidly reviving from frozen isolation;
leased for grazing the broad slopes
above forested canyons and draws cleaving the valley.

Abandoned one-room line shacks,
spread around the elongated valley,
collapsing to disordered log piles
of gray-brown timber, and cement chinking.
Beside one, a rusting steel mowing machine
conceals the tan marmot's den and sanctuary,
winter refuge and spring hideout from interlopers.

The rolling stream, gathering pond runoff and rivulets,
races and tumbles under a rough platform bridge.
Crossing its span, outbound from this reviving ranch,
a jean-jacketed cowhand riding his muscled horse;
working uphill then along the high country's ramshackle line fence.
Two barbed wire strands held upright by makeshift poles,
threading through snow banks and tangled lodgepole pine,
skirting mountain ponds and sidestepping boulders
erupting through tenuous soil.

His mountain horse, iron-shod by a low-country blacksmith,
carefully inserts each hoof through treacherous snowbanks,
moving upslope of outcroppings; ever higher into retreating snow.
The bay gelding's a black mane and tail with three white leggings;
its nostrils running hot and wet from climbing through cold, thin air.
Part thoroughbred, part quarter-horse, tonguing a steel curb bit;
a brown stock saddle cinched tight over its wool blanket
with the horn dally-wrapped using inner tube rubber.
Coiled lariat and small wire rolls lashed to either flank.

Spring's breeze fills the rider's blue jacket;

damp trousers cover pointed leather boots
growing wet from thawing brush.
Red COOP baseball cap, holstered wire cutters
hanging from a tooled leather belt with silver rodeo buckle.
Softening chocolate bar bulges one breast pocket
and green tin of dip tobacco the other.

His current lady housekeeping over summer,
unloading the dull red Dodge pickup:
houseware, bedding, and groceries
packed alongside a plain stock saddle;
all resting flat on its rough wood bed.
Thin sable-haired woman, an agent's wife,
leaving her city house for the cowboy life;
and man who won't know she's gone
until home from the game.

Mountain summer will follow,
then surrender to fall's palette.
Cattle will load out for feedlots,
the summer ranch abandoned,
and meadows left to earth-brown elk
eluding fluorescent-orange hunters;
then winter's isolation and deep snow.

When the spring melt next fills irrigation ditches
scratched across adobe flatland
ski condos and postage-stamp ranches
will have driven cattle from the mountain valley.
Developers serving invading outlanders,
crossing deserts from the West Coast,
or mountains from the East,
to bulldoze a cattlemen and cowboy legacy;
leaving only recalcitrant remnants,
and memories of their passing;
a good way, an American way.

Working Wounded

Hector Jones ambles easy through a chromed door,
passing crowded tables to the padded bar
with drinks scattered below harlequin bottles
and signs twisting on their nylon tethers.

From the white short-sleeved shirt,
his right arm's a long cylindrical stump,
little forearm, no wrist, palm, or fingers;
only ghost sensations deceiving the brain.

Newcomers watch his cautious progress,
easing through the crowd with a broad smile,
favoring the long-healed wound.
Local regulars with longnecks call out,
motioning him to their tables and bar.

City tourists and travelers turn guilt away;
a war casualty returned home,
not yet hidden, buried or etched in granite.
The last war's disfigured and gassed
having conveniently passed,
so new draft boards are convened
and politicos working diligently,
to shield sons, grandsons, and friends.

Once called, the farmer's only son,
rushed to finish fall's corn harvest.
Sawing through that arm with a jackknife
saved his life just before wrist and hand
joined stalks and iron-hard yellow ears,
entering the vibrating corn picker's clawing maw,
beside an idling orange Farmall; so he missed their war.

Eight-ball and a Quarter

Western Slope Friday night always fills one tavern on the short dirt road's turnaround. Set off from its bar are two pool tables with worn green felt streaked by too many balls and chrome slide worn gray. The half-dozen quarters lining a side-rail wait to free its colored balls in a noisy avalanche for the table's cracked, plastic triangle. Brown and faux-ivory pool sticks, some less bent than others, fill a floor stand. Patrons mingle in a bouquet of strong perfume, cigarettes, and beer. Country music blasts from a chrome and multicolored glass jukebox embellished with lariats, six-guns, cowboys, cowgirls, and horses. From outside come the sounds of tires crunching through parking lot pea-stone and radios braying from open windows as approaching headlights pierce glass panes to flash against nondescript paneling inside. Patrons mingle, mill, or sit below fluorescent lights and slow-turning ceiling fans. Some work cattle but most earn frugal livings on surrounding farms, at the dam, or around town.

Two men shoot pool wearing black felt hats, snap-buttoned white shirts, blue jeans, and pointed western boots. The rounder's workshirt will someday go to the feedlot but his opponent's will stay weekends-only. During the rounder's workdays it's ball caps and thinning blue jeans with pockets ringed by Red Man dipping tobacco tins. The rounder's boots lack pointed steel toe-guards since they'll follow his shirt when something more than worn tennis shoes proves necessary at work.

The rounder does extremely well matching his bar stick against a custom cue extracted from its wooden box. Invited outside by the loser, he knows what's waiting. Celebrating a week's hard work dipping cattle and several cold, foamy beers have left him unsteady and right with the world; but sober enough. He declines then joins two young friends while his adversary slow-sips Seagram's in a freshly waxed pickup; knowing few have bested this rounder at work, riding, cattle, fencing, or fighting until booze banderillas lower those broad, thick shoulders.

Several beers later the rounder steps through the door onto parking lot gravel, begins walking towards his ancient GMC flatbed on a pickup chassis, looks into a lever-gun, and hears an angry voice threatening to shoot. Dulled by drink, the rounder growls not to miss or he'll be on him like stink on shit. The muzzle shifts slowly between the rounder and his friends. Those powerful fists double, curious drinkers come outside, and a crowd gathers. The stage is set but an impasse holds, clouded by beer, until the local hero takes a hand.

This part-time constable, beneath the state patrol, sheriff, and city police, trumpets his bona fides, takes charge, and confronts the lever-gun clenching drunk. The crowd stares, an unsteady rounder watches, and his two young friends step away as the rifle cracks once then twice more, each shot separated only long enough to lever fresh rounds. At less than two yards all three strike the hero. One slug passes through the shoulder, a second burrows along his left side, and the third glances off a lower right rib. Anticipating a fourth, the rounder sprints for thick mesquite surrounding road and lot while his friends race for their car then barrel away; spraying the crowd with pebbles before meeting the arriving police cruisers. Roughly extracted and pinned to the hard-packed adobe by shotguns upside heads, one yells, "We're the victims, Gawd dammit."

Dragged back to the lot where a milling crowd includes one stunned hero walking about and the shooter; officers demand this culprit be pointed out but find only silence. The bar crowd may be shocked, cowed, or muzzled but not the fast-sobering rounder. He staggers from the brush, shaking his head and muttering people keep getting him in trouble before spotting the man with custom cue and long gun now returned to the window rack. Towing an officer, he advances, cursing, "I'll point out the son of a bitch." A single blow lands the shooter in dusty pea-stone with a cut lip trickling blood. The dazed hero is also cut from the crowd and slid into an ambulance while the revived assailant is cuffed for an appointment with the judge; then time in Canyon City. Monday finds the rounder back working the feedlot, one young friend irrigating its adobe barley fields, and a tourist no longer claiming the Western Slope lacks excitement. By morning, that small tavern on the short dirt road turnaround has emptied, its windows dark, and pool tables waiting silently for next Friday's silver coins.

Western Slope Sisters

Two Uncompahgre women,
thirty-some years apart;
forty-some miles distant.
Amelia Anne Baumann,
admired by the boys, but never one.
Amanda Anne Mallory,
admired by the boys whose wives shun.

Amelia was never without her red Stetson,
styled white hair, and brown parchment skin
from a lifetime under hot Western Slope sun.
Breasts grown heavy, a thin butt grown broad,
thick waist cinched by a silver rodeo buckle
and tooled leather belt with her name on back.
Once the lithe barrel racer, riding the edge,
never making a slip; taking life the same way.
Dark sunglasses, turquoise jewelry,
and commanding range voice for work or play.
A woman who dabbled, never married though asked,
and drank with the boys at the end of each day.

Office, restaurant, or roadhouse;
desk, chrome barstool, or booth;
drunk, sober, mad, or sad;
she wheeled and she dealt but seldom was had.
Five thousand acres wore this lady's brand,
lush mountain pasture and irrigated flatland.
Born strong on a farm then toughened by strife,
Amelia flew white El Caminos through a remarkable life;
and home with horses, dogs, and cats most every night.

Amanda's long hair was flowing white-blond silk,

lightened and dried under the Western Slope sun.
Features thin and fine; eyes faded sky blue;
maybe forty summers or perhaps twenty-two.
Her loose cotton work shirts often shown through,
their pearly, snap buttons given little to do.
Serious, quiet, determined, and shy;
she constantly pushed to be one of the guys;
but ranching was all that she'd ever try.

The professor's daughter left Berkeley
for Boulder, where she couldn't remain,
so she suddenly crossed the divide,
for the Western Slope's high plain.
Amanda keeps cattle, horses, dogs, and a cat;
and works outdoors with men she attracts.
The Chevrolet truck has racks for the horse,
and gets her about as she sets her own course.

Amelia is envied by farmers, ranchers, bankers, and boys.
Amanda is loathed by every one of their wives.
Respected or not it's always the same,
never choose to be different, stay true to the game,
or take your own path; but dues won't be the same.

Colorado Rounder

Her Colorado rounder rode hard through this life,
old flatbed Chevy, untold girlfriends, three lively wives,
a sixteen-hand gelding, and tan dingo dog.
The Western Slope cowboy only once crossed a divide,
to serve time in Canyon City paying his dues,
after trouncing six deputies and tearing their blues.

His chariot was worn;
dark blue paint faded from sun;
with flowing, art deco lines,
and straight-six engine that most always would run.
Its oiled wood bed kept clear by the wind,
above bald, black dual tires stained by adobe,
a single red taillight, and chromed women mud-flaps.
Beneath a split front window, with small hairline crack,
its chrome radio blares from a painted steel dash.
Round faded instruments; oil, speedo, and tach;
with fender turn-signals that took a full day to attach.
Its single chrome headlights show him the way,
while long, pole side-mirrors whistled joy every day,
as the rounder's blue chariot roared through the flats.

Horsehead spinner clamped to a worn steering wheel,
and floor-shift stalk his strong arms smoothly jammed;
supple boots double-clutching three gears and reverse,
knowing each day was good and could always be worse.
The dingo's wet nose pointed straight into the wind,
tongue trailing behind against ruffling dirty tan fur.
Cocking his head, standing firm with lips in a grin,
behind a dented blue cab at the short bed's front end;
beside a battered toolbox with too many brands,
staring through dusty rear windows while watching his man.

Her rounder loved life, women, and wives;
dogs, stout horses, and too many dives.
Cruising all over in that damned old blue truck;
dark, loving, and rugged, he seemed always in luck,
except when double-timed lovers, grown suddenly wise,
cornered their Colorado rounder gassing his truck.

He broke saddle horses to pay his own way;
fed feedlot cattle grain, molasses, and hay;
or worked high country ranches by month, week, or day.
"Hell of a bunch of hands," he would often say,
then climb in his truck for home; or maybe part way.
No one could best him; field, bar, tavern, or street;
but after libations, weekend cowboys would cheat,
and he'd trade blow for blow while still on his feet.
Hurt far too often but never once cowed,
and mano y mano could never be beat.

Her Colorado rounder cursed and fought his bold bay,
shod hooves against club, clashing day after day;
dust, screams, and thuds but neither would cave.
Riding fence, working cattle, or irrigating the fields,
her rounder's free spirit would not bend, break, or yield.
When that big heart gave out, and his ride reached its end,
there were wives, lovers, women, children, and kin
who loved their old rounder and remembered him when.

His headstone's well-tended.
The truck's left to rust
with vines through its wheels,
behind an empty ranch house
between two alfalfa fields.
The dingo's a memory,
like his quarter-horse bay,
but her Colorado rounder
lived every damned day.

Fatal Misjudgment

Pongo was a dog,
a paperless Dalmatian
with a whimsical name.
The black and white puppy
wrenched from his mother
for the Western Slope;
to find warm security
in the young son's bed,
a new family, and friends.

Pongo was a dog,
a short-haired sire,
who rode every pick-up seat,
bolt-upright, paws forward;
and loved running free.

Pongo was a dog,
who mothered kittens
their molly ignored,
giving warm security
on a carpeted floor;
between long legs
protecting his horde.

Pongo was a dog,
who never fought,
who ran from a Chihuahua,
who fled the tan dingoes,
who ignored their laughing;
choosing flight over fight.

Pongo was a dog,
who crossed the road,
who wandered the feedlot,
who ran when set upon
while trying to be free.

Pongo was a dog,
who fled into a cul-de-sac,
between office and scales,
three barking dingoes
hot on his heels.
Trapped; unable to run,
killed their leader first,
then two more quickly done.

Indigenous Expatriate

No phone calls, no letters;
lost friends in familiar places fade:
too busy, too far, too distant.
A Colorado sun blazing in the clear blue sky
brightens nothing but tall mountains.
A Michigan sun piercing gray clouds,
lights familiar fields and woods.
Hope blossoms and fades,
under the same burning orb;
is this the time, the place, to be?

Hipster Redux

The tourist fled teaching; unable to plod summer-to-summer while keenness dulled. A Chicago bus brought him out of the Upper Peninsula; from that city he hitchhiked to Boulder. Hustling beer on The Hill then a year on the Western Slope left him prey for the rotund navy recruiter so a Convair 580 lifted him back over the peaks to Denver and a hotel Cassidy and Kerouac staggered past scouring Larimer Street. A day spent in its neglected ballroom enlisting before an anxious evening sipping syrupy Black Russians in the blue neon-bathed, Naugahyde and chrome lounge while a woman from another age sang beside its piano.

He shared an overnight room before breakfast on the navy tab with cold November held at bay just beyond the bricks, and large windows with gold stripes. Light snow drifted slowly down from buildings overlooking the broad street; moving irregularly with the breeze before dusting moist concrete. The restaurant with two entrances was a long room off the hotel's entryway that consisted of glass door sets insulating its lobby from outside. One restaurant entrance was through a door from that dead space and the smaller second one opening to the sidewalk was controlled over forty-three years by a muscular bronze door closer. His booth, matching every other against the exterior wall, was midway down, across the narrow aisle from a sparsely occupied counter bisecting the long, narrow space and topped by turquoise linoleum.

His stout, affable waitress penciled the order on her green pad then quickly returned with two eggs up, link sausage, and margarine-damp toast slices. Hot, black coffee in a worn, off-white victory mug followed the fluted plastic glass filled to its chipped rim with pulpy orange juice. He grasped the cup with both hands; enjoying its warmth until cool enough to sip without burning tongue or lips. The food was nearly gone when a figure clutching bundled papers entered; accompanied by a burst of cold air as the slow-closing door allowed snow eddies to spiral above blue-green tile.

Indigent or eccentric, his worn gray suit was well-cut but lacked luster and offered scant protection. Dull silver hair streaked with gray was neatly brushed back from his slightly red forehead; likely by two oval brushes with mother-of-pearl backs. The ragged bundle clutched as though a deacon's bible seemed a musical score worried with longhand notes. Crossing slowly to where wall and counter converged, without looking about, he laid this frayed opus gently on the countertop then, with practiced dignity, slid onto the roughly patched turquoise vinyl of a chrome bar stool with circular foot ring just above the floor. Every movement suggested this was a familiar haunt and that particular stool chosen to ensure more than arms' length separation from other patrons hunched over the counter. The tourist believed the music was jazz, without justification.

The waitress eyed him with disapproval while sliding orders of flaxen-yellow scrambled eggs before men in suits and warm coats; then snapped with feigned irritation, "What do you want? We don't need no bums. If you don't order, you gotta leave."

"Some hot water please, ma'am."

"All right, but we don't allow no bums."

"Yes, ma'am."

After steaming water landed before him with enough momentum to spill over the cup's graying rim, his left hand dipped into a jacket pocket. The emerging tea bag was extracted from its wrapper, waxed string with square tail carefully unwound, and then lowered gently into steaming water. For exactly two minutes it slowly dipped several times with the dedication, control, and intensity of a tea ceremony.

The waitress shifted attention to booth customers, pulled a stainless steel pot from the Bunnomatic, and began rounds. She paused by the tourist, "Freshen your coffee, sir?"

His was still too hot to enjoy without cream and sugar, "No thanks, ma'am."

In a voice intended to carry, she broadcast, "That old bum always comes in about this time."

Man and waitress were of an age and when the tourist proved unreceptive she went to the next booth. Her target ignored the cut and continued sipping as it was revisited at every station along windows overlooking a bleak street. Impervious and detached, he sat quiet and patient beside the opus, concentrating on his insipid tea;

clearly grateful for this morning sanctuary's warmth. After watching the waitress with steaming coffee pot pass by and that steel carafe return to its hot plate, he politely inquired, "Some more hot water if you would, ma'am." Shaking her head, she pulled a different carafe with boiling water and refreshed his tea with a brief remark too quiet for others to overhear.

The tourist finished his coffee while surreptitiously studying the man who said nothing, sipped tea, and intermittently glanced over one shoulder at passing cars and people outside. It all seemed staged; some other time's bleak remnant. The recruit looked outside, speculating how close by old Larimer Street was while streaks of yellow yoke congealed on the dull-white plate and his cup emptied.

Eschewing preliminaries, the man retrieved his bundle, thanked the waitress, and then decamped just as he entered; treating nearby patrons with a second rush of November air. Like an apparition, the gentleman walked down the sidewalk through light blowing snow without revealing a past relationship with this waitress, who he was, his music, or future.

The tourist pushed his worn cup away, noticed black coffee grains staining its bottom, stood up, and walked to the register. A Marine gunnery sergeant was holding his ticket for San Diego's Recruit Training Command. Thanksgiving was less than a week off but he saw no reason to linger. Colorado seemed unusually frigid that year.

A Curious Epoch's Volunteers

Northerners, Southerners, Westerners, and Easterners;
city folk, suburban men, county boys, and foreigners;
blond, brunette, redhead, black, white, yellow, red, brown;
short hair, long hair, balding, tall, short, muscled, and rotund;
wait while sharing a cavernous barracks room with large windows,
heavily waxed floor, metal cots, and blue-gray blankets.
Eating then smoking; eating then napping;
eating then conferring, scheming, bragging, comparing.

Form up in the passage, form up outside, form up on the grinder.
There the unworldly, unemployed, travelers, wanderers,
naivetés, adventurers, 20-year men shuffle uneasily;
standing in ragged ranks on painted concrete.
Young men, not so young men, older men, fathers, sons,
high school graduates, college graduates, and veterans;
different demeanor, appearance, dress, and thought.
Seagulls swoop, soar, and swarm overhead, seeking garbage;
targeting recruits noisily, maliciously, remorselessly.

Their newly mustered company ambles off;
to the barber shop where equality starts,
to the storehouse where uniforms are issued,
to the building where clothes and personal items go home,
to the mess-hall where its nut-to-butt with five minutes to eat,
to the barracks where uniforms are stowed and head scrubbed.
Only the person remains, the individual, the man.

Fred was an Air National Guard boot,
Darius ran with the Blackstone Rangers,
Joel soldiered in Vietnam,
John was a teacher,
Jose earned a master's degree in Manila,

Jim was fired from the supermarket,
Tom could never decide,
Terry left Toledo's streets,
Rick wanted something not the suburbs,
Arthur wanted something not the farm,
Ed wanted college tuition,
Jerry is guaranteed a school.
Sam sees an achievable future.
Most want travel but few the sea.

Records reviewed, people observed, selections made;
best marcher, recruit chief petty officer;
best guess leader, recruit first class petty officer;
best guess manager, company yeoman;
best guess boss, master at arms;
until graduation, failure, replacement, or drop.

March in formation to eat,
march in formation to fill out forms,
march in formation to class,
march in formation to get shots,
march in formation to the pool,
march in formation to inspection,
march in formation to church.
A moving, fledgling male fraternity in formation.

Some fail tests and leave,
some give up and drop,
some are sick and set back,
some find trouble and go home,
some should not get through but might,
most press forward, day and night.

Fold clothes right,
polish brass bright,
slip cigarettes in socks,
dry shave furtively,
shine shoes at night,
drill with Springfield rifles of 1903,

envy Marines across the fence,
run obstacle course...once,
survival swimming...once,
walk the beached ship mock-up.

Graduation day and freedom,
to the buses and then away.
It's finally over,
off to ship or school,
back to the bottom,
but willing to climb,
and reach the top;
shipmates of a curious epoch.

Into the Bay

A gray frigate eases down Kennebec River, passes Pond Island, and leaves Maine for January's white and gray bay. Her bulging stem makes its first plunge, then more growing increasingly violent. The long forecastle is submerged and bow thrust up; hurling saltwater against already encrusted bridge windows. These tortured contortions repeat endlessly. Bow and keel hang naked over deep troughs before crashing down; yawing as they cut deep into cold, heaving water. Four thousand tons suddenly lift, shudder, drop, shudder, and repeat. Her groaning hull rolls side-to-side with fin stabilizers that catch, struggle, and return. The hull bucks fifty times to expel 5-inch rounds.

Prostrate forms in pungent chambray shirts and dungarees layer the forward head's gray terrazzo deck; groaning in weak protest while enduring their saltwater miasma and the damp vomit stench. Wretched khaki victims above are also hors de combat in cramped, gyrating staterooms. On or off watch, bilious sailors dry heave through purgatory. Her tall, thick whip antennas, sway, snap, and vanish overboard in the black night during a midwatch too nauseous to notice or care. Bay of Fundy winters distress green crews or sailors too long ashore; and Bath Iron Works still two days off.

Evening Chimerical

Cars crammed in the diminutive lot
outside a cement block building,
across from McDonald's and Wendy's.
Men converge from base, work, university, and home
in shirts and jackets of leather, twill, or cotton;
single, engaged, married, and divorced.

Beyond its dull, painted steel door
a fleeting sham experience;
beer on tap, beer in bottles, wine in glasses.
An honest establishment where ladies,
won't drink light wine then charge champagne;
but gyrate on a small corner stage,
before lap dancing between round tables.

Casually dressed women,
carrying large shoulder bags
pass unmolested through patrons;
swallowed by the arena dressing room,
beyond another doorway's thick drape
past a short bar and its impervious tender.
Street clothes vanish,
halters fitted, G-strings pulled in place;
hand-sewn to patterns or the lady's design;
using high school skills from the year before
or a decade past; and real dancing shoes for some.

Practice, practice, practice every routine,
in trailers, apartments, and rented homes;
gyrating to blaring stereos and record players.
Preparation to mount the cramped stage by rote
and face a blurred public beyond its bright lights.

Bare-breasted lap dancers working tables pause,
hands fall to hips; professional courtesy
while judging their evening's competition.
Waitresses earn wages,
but dancers are entrepreneurs;
so every stage performance
determines the night's take at tables.

Janette emerges from dressing room,
summoned by the manager.
Heavy breasts, wide hips, and red hair,
gyrating to *Hit Me With Your Best Shot*.
Single mother, divorced at nineteen,
and part-time waitress.

Lucinda steps up from waiting tables;
rail thin with firm implants,
and cosmetology her life's desire.
The small, silk top comes away,
to *Right Down the Line*.
Low murmur of appreciative applause;
while she looks forward to the apartment
shared with a high school boyfriend.

Jean's their seasoned trooper.
Six years on the Flint production line
ignoring, diverting, and fending off men
for free on the factory floor until it closed;
then migrating south for work,
where she now struts to *Barracuda*.

Sheryl craved attention since a babe,
a short brunette with hourglass figure,
soaking up smiles, stares, and applause.
Slowly flexing under hot lights,
masked by drifting cigarette smoke,
with *Stairway to Heaven* adding fantasy.

Norma's neither pretty nor friendly,

but the room grows silent each time,
Karma Chameleon brings her to the stage.
A chiseled figure and sensuous presence,
intimidating aficionados she cares nothing for;
but welcomed by sisters after working the floor.

Karen sweats heavily in hot lighting,
revolving to *The Tide Is High*;
remembering the days at sea
on her father's shrimp boat,
the young men spurned,
and the one she chose.
Alone with a daughter, no man,
and cheap shrimp from foreign lands.

Mary's young and serious,
engaged to the sailor she adores,
deployed on a haze-gray oiler;
while she writhes innocently through
Keep On Loving You.
Intense but true, she refuses men
at her apartment door,
and knows just what to do.

Some will marry, some will not,
some will remember, a few may not,
some will be grandmothers, some not,
some will be happy, others not,
some will be addicts, most will not,
some will succeed, some will not;
a short gig for some but others it's not.

The Last Port Call

A house and home transformed;
sited on Nassau's crowded slope
above the vanished pirate fortress.
Now an international pub
looking out over city rooftops
to the crystalline blue harbor,
docked cruise ships, and solitary gray frigate.

Long bar running down on one side
below its large mirror and shelved bottles;
varnished floorboards worn smooth;
wood pillars replacing solid walls,
supporting overhead beams and rafters.
Background music fills this painted surround;
driving its steadily drinking crowd to loud intimacy
in English, German, French, and Caribbean.
Tourists? Travelers? Vacationers? Vagabonds?
Young men, young women, Caribbean characters.
Comradeship, relationships, dialogue, intercourse.

One last gin and tonic then a gaily decked-out cab
and across the lighted brow before liberty expires;
ending this fleeting, too perfect Caribbean idyll.
Can a sailor return? Can time stop?
Norfolk and discharge in seven days.

Friends, Companions, and Shipmates

Tis neither me nor thee
but we, and they, and us;
close, far, dead, and gone.
Time passes and all must change;
accepting whatever the mind retains,
until all that never was remains.

Paris Nocturne

When he last saw Paris,
city parks were vibrant green,
stone boulevards gray and damp.
The confined Seine flowed gently
past cane-pole fishermen
under ancient stone arches
as spring's breath caressed outdoor cafes
and their bustling wrought-iron tables.

When he last saw Paris,
there were Hemingway, Fitzgerald,
Twysden, Stein, and Pound.
Only fantômes remain.
He'll not see that Paris again;
did any of them?

Key West Adieu

He loved Key West,
and a wrecker's house.

He loved Key West,
with rum-running conchs.

He loved Key West,
of black, brown, yellow, and white.

He loved Key West,
through a depression's dark days.

He loved Key West,
but no longer around,
when affluent condo creatures,
rode his one true world down;
then prancing drunk through its streets
came party-hearty clowns.

A Mazatlán Night

Mexican street vendors
bivouac on a Pacific night's shore;
greet and succor gringo tourists
sleeping under thin beach towels,
shivering in the cool night breeze;
waiting for their morning train north.

Heilbronn Woods

Off serpentine black asphalt
climbing forested hills above Heilbronn,
beyond the white Trappensee Castle
and lines of green vineyards,
where cars line a gravel shoulder
feeding one tamed forest portal.

Sunlight filtering through trees,
light an old man's walk,
his beloved dog unleashed,
pawing leaf piles; sniffing and talking.

The bitch scampers about,
staying close by her master,
barking temporary freedom,
avoiding water and mud,
exploring worn dirt paths.
She relieves, sniffs at grass tufts,
and alerts to chirping birds
concealed in multi-colored leaves.

The schnell frau jogs past
in gray flannel running suit;
down the trail, across a fire lane,
below a shooting tower to cull gentle deer.

The sprechen frau stops,
warm in down jacket and hat,
putting off her inescapable return
to an upstairs city apartment
where she lives alone.

Woodland circuit complete,
dog coaxed into a blue Volvo,
the old man returns home;
his dog barking satisfaction
from the station wagon's rear seat.

A Dubious Hunt

The high-country park lays tranquil.
Tourists have retreated to cities,
summer grazing cattle to feedlots.
Elk sense the change,
know its meaning,
drift slowly to deep cover.

Bulls, cows, and yearlings
seeking food, water, and safety
ghost wary, silent, and invisible
through slopes, woodlands, and clear-cuts;
crossing fire roads and underbrush,
jumping downed fence lines,
sensing past seasons' losses,
fearing another hard winter,
feeling approaching snow.

Local hunters and guides
track their movements
through field glasses,
study droppings,
scout before their hunt.
Some hope to fill winter larders,
others to earn a guide's pay.

Light brown elk;
fewer than deer,
larger than deer,
more elusive than deer;
so stalkers' tempers smolder and flare,
when sweeps prove fruitless.

Heavy canvas wall-tent,
filling a gentle depression
along the cold mountain stream
below a steep asphalt road.
The fire pit cleared of pine needles,
safely distant from pickup and trailer
with tires crusted in frozen mud.

Brisk morning, warm coffee,
then hunting upslope
into pine and aspen forest;
hiking some forgotten roadbed.
Narrow gauge rails long since salvaged;
only creosote ties remain,
misaligned and scattered
by time, snow, saplings, and trees.

Abandoned lumber mill, rising above the flats,
sunbeams striking a graying skeleton,
further exposed as rough pine boards fall
near shrinking sawdust piles.
Its companion ghost town
small, unused, boarded buildings
along the asphalt state road;
marked by faded signs:
no trespassing; no dumping.

Bulky, florescent orange vest,
reassuring nylon backpack,
filled with water, food, and maps.
Classic bolt-action rifle,
iron sights and smooth, polished wood;
its heavy-bellied rounds from a war to end all wars.

Trekking through cold stillness,
laced boots clutching ankles,
feet cold, hands numbing;
but alone, independent,
accepting primeval risk

in the mountain forest.
Skirting a forgotten gravel pit,
with stones and rocks laid bare,
stripped of trees, plants, and topsoil.

Lunch on a damp log, warmed by the sun,
sipping cold water, chewing tangy jerky,
salty nuts, and sweet, dried pineapple.
Summer's insects sound final chirps,
squirrels and chipmunks scamper,
feeding trout disturb a ponding creek,
blackbirds cry shrilly, intermittently,
as woodpeckers tap, tap, tap.
Stillness, silence, no people, no talk, no noise,
only sounds of a thousand years past.
A cautious deer pauses, slakes its curiosity,
flashes across the open between cover,
bounding over recent bear droppings
standing proud amongst drying deer pellets,
and elk leavings.

Pungent venison cooking on a wood fire.
Hunters returned from mountain or blind,
gather in warmth, heat, and smoke.
Night comes while they speak;
planning their next day, the coming year,
reminiscing their past, considering the future.
One bull elk watches from cloaking timbers above,
before lumbering off with two cows and three yearlings;
to face winter's snow and survive.

The Green Glass Bowl

Translucent green fruit bowl;
thick glass hemisphere
on round brass base.
Proud on the store shelf
until wrapped in paisley pink paper
for their classmates' wedding.

Empty most of the first year,
fruit and nuts in season,
then filled with bills, letters, and jotted notes.
Proud on kitchen counter
as a child crawled then walked past.

Filled while decades pass;
fruit and nuts in season,
or bills, letters, notes, and small articles.
Packed for a cottage
when four became two, then one.

Unnoticed for a year,
without fruit or nuts.
Bills, letters, and notes forgotten.
Proud on a closet shelf
while another decade passed,
before progeny return.

Removed one last time
as two grown children watch
youth's green icon
cross the auction table;
clearing a small, cloistered room
for another reluctant inmate.

Translucent green fruit bowl,
a thick glass hemisphere,
on round brass base.
Proud and dusty on the store shelf
before wrapping in brown paper.
Reclaimed by the bewildered man
who grew old around it years before.

The Heretic

A wandering tourist,
stopped to ask the way,
while walking a familiar path;
claiming he was led astray.

Everyone asked how that could be
with leaders' signs for all to see.
Exasperated, sad, and mad he screamed,
"We're all lost and you can't just be!"

Humanity

Life's stream flows slowly,
through each and every being,
mutating constantly,
shaped by social contrivance,
until emerging manipulated and scarred,
from humanity's imperfect mold.

A Place We've Never Been

Fragmentary retreats to childhood,
longing for past youth's world,
wishing for that perfect place;
those faultless times;
when all was happy, peaceful, and fine.
These never were and will never be;
whether theirs, ours, yours, or mine.

Somewhere Out West

Hitch'n in to Frisco,
met an aging railroad bum.
Through stained and absent teeth,
he laughed off everyone.
I faced him, he faced me.
You're a bum I cried!
Brown tobacco juice arced
across the rusting rails;
isn't everyone he sighed?

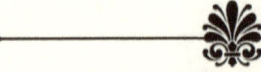

Street Philosopher's Demise

Alone in the switchyard,
amongst rusting rails and broken ties,
a dying hobo stared at his winter's sky.
He laughed, he spit, and sipped
brown-sacked Thunderbird wine.
Saying this here bottle's all I got,
but what I have is mine.
Ain't go'n nowhere special,
never went nowhere fast,
so my only aspiration's
to make this moment last.

Late Summer Idyll

Lively green leaves,
fading to fall's many hues,
rustling from Indian Summer's
caressing wind;
fall gently, noiselessly
on the woodland pond
to float sedately
above grasping mud.
Green frogs leap matted grass,
a doe feeds in silent peace
as universes slip past.

Beyond the Crossroad

Agnes Carrie was born
in a fieldstone farmhouse;
off the asphalt road to town,
beside a white, hip-roof barn,
with roofless brown-tile silo.
Her town faded to village;
four-way stop, one general store,
three churches, two gas stations,
vacant buildings, and post office.

Agnes Carrie was left alone
when her husband passed;
living in a white clapboard house
by the white church and brick gas station
at the red light flashing overhead.
Her fieldstone basement,
enclosed a congenial village store,
marked by the simple wood sign
strung across a broad oak's crotch.
Three rows of second-hand shelves
under a low, whitewashed ceiling,
crammed with food, snacks, and sundries.
In the rear, a wonderfully cluttered counter;
its out-sized antique brass register
surrounded by penny candy, treats, and gum.

Agnes Carrie stayed open late,
gossiping with her neighbors
buying small items and snacks.
Everyone loved her smile,
everyone loved her laugh;
except three fledgling urban thugs.

Agnes Carrie's face was struck,
her fallen body kicked and beaten,
for fifty dollars and three Mars bars.
Each misunderstood youth
received six months' probation,
and their second chance.

Agnes Carrie felt isolated and ignored;
never again well and seldom laughed.
Her store shut and shelves emptied;
that basement door closed forever;
locked to friends, neighbors, and strangers.

Agnes Carrie died,
before three probations ended,
and buried before three arrests
for another store and worse;
yet aging children remember
those summer nights,
cozy basement store,
and its ebullient mistress.

A Spinster Aunt

Her numbered parking spot,
stands empty and neglected
under spring's bright sun,
reflecting off glossy black asphalt
between rows off townhouses;
puddled from overnight rain.
One empty basement garage waits
beside a miniature, flowered yard,
now two weeks unattended.

Her absence announced
by a small printed sign;
impaled in moist earth
at the complex entrance;
attracting merely curious
and genuine customers.
Rummaging treasure seekers
hope shoes and pasteboard boxes
conceal overlooked jewelry.
Placards are taped to the door;
one welcoming all,
the other warning all sales final.

Her comfortable, secure redoubt;
the bright, well-ordered home,
a twenty-year refuge,
with clean ivory walls,
noise deadening carpets;
and air not yet stale or musty
from abandonment.

Her waiting double bed, precisely made;

its cream coverlet left taut
when she quit for two days in hospital;
now strewn with shoes, purses, and clothes.
The nightstand's plain-framed photo
taken for a Chicago magazine.
A middle-aged lady with short, dark hair.
Perhaps one who clawed up a career pyramid;
but maybe daughter, niece, or absent companion.
Paintings, drawings, prints, and etchings
of animals, designs, and landscapes
hung carefully throughout the floors;
but none of family, people, or lovers.

Her round oak table, absent two leaves,
displays wrist watches and jewelry;
the heavy, ornate, and costume
favoring dark, formidable women.
Small piles of fussy art deco
bracelets, necklaces, earrings, rings;
all large and gaudy curiosities
lacking pearls, silver, or gold.
Everything passed down from her mother
or accoutrements bought for the office.

Her robin-egg blue couch against the wall;
near the narrow, square-paneled wood door
opening to a dwarf balcony above the parking lot;
overlooking townhouses then stilled lake inlet.
Now occupied by two uninvited, unfamiliar women;
legs up and crossed, fingering I-phones,
oblivious to subdued music encouraging
strangers buying bits of an extinguished life;
ignorant of any item's value or story.

Her entrance closet by the front door,
crowded with faux fur coats,
patent leather shoes, and nylon scarfs;
exposed for view, displaying wares;
like bedroom closets pregnant with clothing;

and stairwell climbing from the entrance;
lined by novelty signs and mélange of items
propped against plasterboard walls.
An idle walker stands ready
alongside walking canes
and small pedal exercise machine.

Her basement room's bookshelves
still embrace Emily Dickinson, Robert Frost,
Voltaire, and Edna St. Vincent Millay.
Beyond its sliding glass door and bulged screen,
the small patio and fenced yard nestle against a hill;
ravaged by winter, muddied from rain;
the few grass shoots beaten to submission
and starved of sunshine by overhead trees.
Dead leaves mix with neglected flowers,
encircling a white café table and two wire chairs;
where she, and for many years they,
enjoyed coffee, croissants, and conversation;
every morning the two were given.

Her kitchen overlooking that backyard,
no longer ordered and pristine;
cluttered with grandmother's china,
exposed for meandering punters.
Disbelieving appliances wait, anticipating her return,
beside the emptied, cleaned, and taped refrigerator.
The almond phone on her light slate countertop;
obscured amidst thick glass and crystal vases;
water-stained from hurriedly discarding flowers;
left wanting cleaning and fresh, green stems.

Her companion's room,
kept its single bed
to serve as couch;
facing the stereo console
and piled record jackets.
Three worn photo albums
spread open on the table.

Black and white snapshots
from the small Illinois school, town, and home
before Saigon and Da Nang.
Places and comrades;
passed on or long forgotten;
treasured and separate from a distant family.

Her upstairs bathroom door
with masking tape-crosses,
matches another beside the garage
filled with tools spread over concrete.
Its red Mercury Cougar's gone,
along with that vanished marque;
a brand she remained loyal to
since Southeast Asia.
Last of its line,
lovingly maintained
well past her ability to drive;
gone to a grandniece,
wanting something newer.

Her frugal life's investments;
eighty years' accumulation;
stocks, bonds, and bank accounts
stripped to pay death taxes.
When the polished brown casket's lowered,
what remains is for her sister's daughter;
issue of the sibling she ignored,
fought, and loved over a lifetime.

Her refuge, home, townhouse is sold;
a recent divorcee with two children coming.
When today's sale completes,
and its residue dumped or donated,
her world and story vanish.
No biography, no autobiography,
only a hurried hometown obituary;
read by the few remembering a young woman.

Her intimate letters burned;
erasing all she knew, lived, and loved.
Everything valued and held dear
forgotten, mangled, sold, and gone.
Stray remnants without understanding;
disconnected bits recalled by families
browsing fading, unlabeled pictures
that fascinate young children
wanting to learn about their spinster aunt
who lived, loved, and passed before their time.

Passages

Love's final, true understanding
comes not at first sight,
or time together, apart,
happy, sick, or sad;
but when forever lost.

Winter's Approach

Drowsing on the canvas recliner
under an Indian Summer sun.
Chipmunks stealing the birds' seeds,
squirrels burying fall's nuts,
wrens fluttering past slowing eyes.
Wool blanket cloaking body and soul
as sunlight filters through quivering trees;
and peaceful days pass without purpose.
Warm winds caress a weathered face,
ruffling thin hair and neglected green grass,
while watching time and life slowly pass.

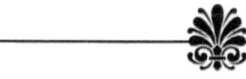
Prelude

He lay in a good bed, shaped and framed by hand, with an oak scent escaping through layers of clear varnish, and mattress good enough. One quack suggested the daughter empty his gun cabinets. Nurses address him like a child; unlike the housekeeper who still cleans every other day. Unable to rise and open latched windows at night; longing for winter's chill outside his warm comforter with its cool breath brushing a white-stubble beard. Every morning becomes less welcome as another long, empty night passes.

Incubus

Night's spasmodic terrors;
a past's nocturnal visits;
unconscious visions rising;
real, conjured, or insane.
Acts unconsummated;
banished, forever lost,
put away before waking.
Return to sentience;
slow and easy,
or through sweaty panic.
In the struggle to wake
blessed are those who succeed.

Lewy Body

Tranquility extinguished by a surreal world.
Those who passed or never were
appear, return, welcome, speak, discuss, and live.
Flashes of another orbit, uncontrollable, unstable.
Fleeting phantoms on floor, bed, and chair;
or walking rooms, peering through doors and windows;
crossing fields, hiking the woods, playing lawn croquet.

Days and nights rich with phantom gargoyles;
long-gone relatives, children, parents, friends;
defying reality, sanity, time, and space.
Escaping thoughts: false, true, or neither.
The never said, never believed;
unmeant, uncontrolled, untrue;
hurting the real, the living, the loved.

A soul slowly wasting
and body loathing itself;
violated, outraged, dispirited.
Undiagnosed, ridiculed, and shunned;
reaching for reality's rote motions,
until drugs close chapter, book, and being;
on a loving man, a kind man, a fine man;
releasing him and freeing an aged love.

A Tenuous State

Curiosity's remorseless seed
lies dormant in the mind.
Should it slip tenuous shackles,
sundry doubts are sown
during an intermittent journey
of sparse, faltering tourists
finding thought insecurity
uncomfortably intoxicating.

This incurious bland valley
in daunting mountains' shadow
defended by unbroken tissue walls;
intellectual cataracts,
shielding contented enclaves,
from threats prowling those slopes.

Complacent schools, towns, villages,
spread across this conforming valley
where gallows wait on village squares
for misdemeanor iconoclasts
with censors' halters swinging
gently in temperate breezes;
impatient to dispatch madmen
who acknowledge rusty tissue scissors
scattered across this contented ground.
Touching brings exile, and lifting death.
Anything to guard cloister, security, and faith.

Strange creatures prowl rising foothills
wander those intimidating mountains;
drift aimlessly and act impulsively.
The tissue wall remains stretched taut

between cardboard fortifications,
casting long, gray shadows
over this pedestrian terrain.
Eager guards on parapets,
swing diatribes overhead;
longing to be the paladin
delaying truth and reality's
constant, inexorable advance.
Irresistible parallels and saps
undermining the lamentable escarpments
shielding this conforming valley.

Beware cerebral wanderers,
probing for weakness;
or catapulting overhead
on bloodied, bleating wings;
penetrating this constrained realm.
Their laughing cries
seeking the most vulnerable
to curiosity's poison.
Terrifying intruders
disrupting blind complacency
propped by toothpick braces
of those forever unquestioning.

Never open up to them,
never venture on those unpredictable slopes,
never wonder what lies beyond the curtain.
Strike down outsiders, doubters, questioners.
Defend, control, and purge this conforming valley;
question nothing; forsake all doubts;
dissonance is subversive;
resist the inevitable no matter the cost.

Sisyphus, Prometheus, and the Tourist

A red Reo fire engine flashes past
three deserted city blocks ahead;
its clanging bell quickly trailing off.
A white Hudson ambulance follows,
leading a running, clamoring pack,
then complete stillness, absolute silence.

The tourist jogs after the cavalcade.
Tennis shoes beat silently on concrete.
No other traffic, pedestrians, or people;
only empty buildings, deserted streets.
All life, sounds, and smells blanched
from this hushed, monochrome metropolis.

Feeling beat beside a small park.
Sit to rest; breathing labored.
No person or creature in sight.
Excitement fades; heart slows.
Lost bearings in a familiar place?
Uncomfortable, unthreatened, uneasy
in these sterile, pregnant surroundings.

Where from? Where going? Who?
Nothing remembered before the fire engine.
Living the moment but no more;
Unknown past, future blank.
Grass covering park flawed
so no satisfaction in reclining.
What's happening? What next?
Look about; disoriented, adrift?

Transparent sky an infinity deep;

too blue, unreal, without clouds.
Tan mountains beyond city skyline.
Dark silhouette descending from their peaks
steadily coming closer, closer, closer.
Twin-engine low-winged monoplane;
one wing tilts lower. Banking or in distress?
Sunlight flashes off riveted aluminum skin.
Windows form a dark stripe down its fuselage.
Staggering as if pilot cannot decide;
land, climb, dive, glide, or jump?
Port radial engine faltering, trailing smoke.
It will soon crash; pilot must be fighting panic.

Glistening nose aims at tourist.
Escape, must escape. Where? How?
Several short sprints, bobs, and weaves.
Plane follows, adjusting, aiming, tracking.
Escape, must escape. Where? How?
Run, run . . . run to where?
Plane closes, blurred people behind windows.
Panic, crying, shock, then acceptance.
"Death travels in that plane. No, God, no!
Go away. Don't take me, too!"

Pilot recovers, gains altitude, banks steeply;
circling towards distant, tan mountains
then gradually turning back towards the city.
Tourist struck with feeling for those near extinction.
Crash taking too long; impatient twisted tenseness.
Get it over, get it over, get it over with.
They're gone. Nothing to be done. Nothing possible.
Never saw a plane crash.

Pilot suddenly banks; altering silhouette,
turning back towards tourist and descending.
Can't be. Retribution? Didn't mean it.
Push the yoke forward;
end this pursuit, this torment, this purgatory.
They must fear crossing alone.

Aircraft expands; dwarfing gray buildings.
Your time, not mine; run, run, run . . ..
Escape, must escape!

Pilot recovers and regains altitude, a few yards,
then flashes overhead, just above flat rooftops,
passing behind gray, austere buildings.
Steep bank and return. Another pass?
Feels as though forever fleeing.
Everything else blotted out.
Don't stumble. Don't fall. Why me?
Your time, not mine; run, run, run . . ..
Escape, escape, must escape!

Pilot recovers; circles wide before returning.
Sun flashes from aluminum wings.
Chance to rest. Tired. Scared.
Pounding heart. Triphammer pulse. Dry throat.

Pilot begins a final approach;
flaps down, left turn, another left, kill engine,
propellers feathered, slow flight, nose up.
Smoke streaming from port engine
staining the blue sky; still infinite and cloudless.

Pilot levels before descending into the vacant metropolis.
Landing gear extends slowly from wings then locks;
will glide over a street several blocks ahead,
making for another vest-pocket park.
Impossible. Too small for landing;
hemmed in by streets and buildings.
Impossible, but nowhere else.
No more delay. Hope they make it.
Still no other people in sight.
Fire engine and ambulance?
Is this where they rushed to?
Who are they? Where are they?

Rapidly descending airplane overshoots park;

slowly sinking somewhere ahead.
Pale passengers, frozen, peer from windows;
some stare enviously towards the ground;
others look away in despair.

Rending, screeching, tearing
several blocks up.
Dull, muffled explosion;
burnt clay bricks clatter across street.
Run towards wreckage and smoke.
Can't be more than three or four blocks.
Relief. It will no longer target those on the ground.
Must see wreck. Nothing like this will happen again.
Streets deserted. May be first. May become a hero?
My wreck. Must reach it before anyone else.
Second and smaller explosion.
More red bricks clatter across concrete.
Two blocks more. Tired. Can't stop.
Not more than a cross-street left.

No wreckage where it should be;
but something two blocks further on.
A silver wingtip thrusts into the street.
Must get there first. Begin jogging.
A red traffic light flashes its demand.
Frustrating. Must see WALK signal to cross.
No traffic and nobody to see violation.
Break the law? What if caught?
If so they can help. Can't decide.
Light turns green.

Leave sidewalk; race towards crash.
Plane rests nose-down in cinder-bricks;
debris scattered over empty blacktop lot.
Different plane entirely. Impossible.
Bent prop on nose, buckled fuselage, twisted empennage.
Mostly intact, washboarded aluminum skin,
no shredding, no scorching, no leaking oil,
no aviation gas vapor, no evidence of fire.

Burnt bricks, clawed asphalt, and dry concrete
under fine gray dust; undisturbed for weeks.
Must be the same plane.
Can't explain. Complete absurdity.

The silent man stands beyond wreckage;
nonchalant, considering the scene;
hands deep in bib overall pockets;
slowly shifting weight between feet.
Cross under empennage to him.
He watches, says nothing,
then returns to studying the crash.
Approach him, breathless, speech difficult,
"What's happening? Anyone alive?"

He turns slowly from studying the plane.
Sorrowful, sun-wrinkled face; vacant eyes.
A slow shrug; hands buried in pockets.
No one else in sight. Just two people and victims.
"Have you checked inside? Did you call for help?"
Why just stand there?
Another slow, lackadaisical shrug.

Climb a jumbled brick slope to cabin,
Pause to glance over the shoulder.
"Damn you, some may live."
He shrugs once more then reluctantly follows.
Begin clearing bricks blocking sprung hatch.
Pulling together opens lightweight, squealing door.
The small cabin mimics an automobile interior.
Bench seats without harnesses.
Forward windows clear; others clouded.
Diffused light reflecting off small flecks of drifting dust.

The silent man remains outside;
hands braced on doorframe.
Four silent souls inside; sitting upright,
heads cocked over seat backs,
mouths open to mohair headliner.

Father's gray hair curls slightly
above neck rolls.
Mother's rises in a stringy, red bouffant
from recent permanent.
Little girl's in ponytails,
wearing fluffy pink dress and ribbon.
Little boy's in a crewcut,
wearing striped polo-shirt, shorts, tennis shoes.
Reach out and touch man's neck.
Should be dead; all should be dead.
Never felt the dead; is a corpse really stiff? Cold?
Check for pulse; same for others.
All these silent souls unconscious.
Pull them from plane?
Could that injure them?
Should they be on their backs?
Move them? Do something.
Retreat through cabin.

The silent man backs from door frame.
"They're barely alive what should we do?"
He shrugs a third time then leans against wing root,
both hands deep in blue overall pockets.
Concrete roadway searing from sun.
Can't lay survivors on it.
Black, straight-eight Buick sedan,
waiting across the street.
Ignition keys and fob in pocket will fit.

The silent man says nothing;
helps carry survivors to Roadmaster.
Mohair interior, cavernous rear seat.
Load them in same positions as before;
sitting with heads cocked over seatbacks.
All appear napping. No change.
Stupid shifting them but complete now.

Lock car doors, crack windows;
send silent man to call for help.

He shrugs again, scratches head, shuffles off.
Expect he'll not return soon; if ever.
Begin search for another phone in opposite direction.
Best not be long away or another will take credit.
Unlikely; souls locked in car not easily seen.
Everyone must know who rescued them.

People suddenly reappear; not outside, not on the street;
behind a hazy display window in cinder brick drugstore.
Enter through its narrow screen door;
washed out wood with rusted sash spring closer
spanning two bent nails in parched frame.
Slanted wood blocks wedge substantial inside door open.
Cramped interior, well-stocked and friendly.
Narrow aisles beyond pyramided soup-can display.

Lady suddenly sorties from behind the soda fountain;
her body revealing then blocking a black wall phone.
A formidable specter approaching rapidly.
Flimsy print cotton dress brushing wood floor.
Stringy red hair resisting all discipline.
Contorted, freckled face screaming.
Tourist can't comprehend this assault.
"Ma'am; must use telephone.
A plane crashed in the parking lot down the street."
"Don't backtalk me. Will put the cops on you again."
Pulls a steel spade from a floor stand;
advancing, eyes bright, swinging it in wide swaths.

Sprint for door; hit it hands forward.
Burst into street. Screen door strikes wall.
Sash spring brings it shut with flat crack.
Shaken. No explanation. No understanding.
Still recalling nothing before the fire engine.
What if people left in Roadmaster are like her?
Why continue? No one cares. Must return.
Rough burning concrete felt through white tennis shoes.
Turn corner. Comatose survivors appear unchanged.
Suddenly frustrated. Despondent. Jaded.

The silent man leans against one black fender
beside chromed ornamental exhaust ports;
still seemingly devoid of passion or urgency.
"Did you get through to the hospital?"
He replies slowly, quietly, with clear disinterest,
"Yup. Spoke with'em."
Help is coming. Relief. Family will be saved.
"How long?"
"Said they was busy. Should git here next week."

Impossible. Insane. Nothing makes sense.
Tourist eschews resolution, credit, acclaim, asks,
"Who am I, where am I, what am I?"
Begins walking away, moving slowly down the street
though a metropolis steeped in Sunday's lethargy.

A red Reo fire engine flashes past
three deserted city blocks ahead;
its clanging bell quickly trailing off.
A white Hudson ambulance follows,
leading a running, clamoring pack,
then complete stillness, absolute silence.

The Hemingway Organ

The pungent, spindly vagabond specter
with unkempt, stubble beard, battered hat,
and desperately appealing outstretched thumb,
scores his ride from the passing tourist.

At the noir, monochrome row-house
with chalking lead paint, faded colors,
and loose translucent panes in splintered frames;
he cajoles that tourist through its four-panel door
with paint peeling from thirsty, cracked wood.
The visitor passes a haggard woman,
replies to her plaintive, sullen greeting,
crosses over dark, thin-planked oak floors,
moving beyond her three-child pack;
grasping, playing, fighting.
The gaunt, reclining feline queen
licks soft paws with sharp, pointed claws,
suckling a litter of no interest to their tom;
out searching for some available molly.

The vagabond vanishes into a back room;
leaving his benefactor to this Stygian chamber.
A tableau of depression pervades,
revulsion descends, walls close in.
There is no escaping the mute mother,
surrounded by three boisterous gamins
she neither claims, wants, nor loves;
as the youngest pumps a steaming yellow stream,
that puddles and spreads over floor boards.

She retreats to more congenial squalor,
gaunt, sunken eyes inviting the tourist,

to share her lukewarm repast;
tasteless gruel with thin, bland tea.
Organ music, constant and repetitive,
flows softly from the portentous room
that swallowed her man.

The Hemingway organ's siren song,
and hieratic beat coaxing man along,
until ephemeral memories have gone.

She implores the bemused tourist.
Help her flee the music and man
lost to soft, seductive sounds
emanating from the back room.
That low-ceilinged chamber,
tempting men to enter, listen,
then fail their returning.

She must escape a mate obsessed,
return to her kith and kin.
An appalled tourist acquiesces,
walks her across the street,
to safety in the outside night.
A brightly glowing streetlamp
creating shades of black, gray, and white
turns her rough tunic blood red;
the apostate's shaming hue;
disdaining her man, fearing escape.

She freezes, refuses to advance,
bolts away; dragging the tourist,
maneuvering him into the back room.
Tall, ebony organ on rusted casters,
frozen to that spot for decades,
worn ivory keys, black and white,
vibrate to a calypso man's supple hands,
below roving eyes and jaunty straw hat.

The Hemingway organ's siren song,

and hieratic beat coaxing man along,
until ephemeral memories have gone.

The tourist listens closely without effect,
until the rhythms and mystifying beat,
sweep him to the Havana nightclub
where tropical players in evening dress
sip sweet, true, Haitian sugarcane rum.
Men crowd along its leathered chrome bar.
Talk and posture; posture and talk.
Who will stand and who might balk?
Who's best not to cross?
Who's got it and who has not?
Who'll kill clean or decline the shot?

The Hemingway organ's siren song,
and hieratic beat coaxing man along,
until ephemeral memories have gone.

The mesmerized tourist wavers.
Fearfully considering woman, kids, and cats.
Must bring her out; bring them all out.
She escapes to his car under the streetlight;
then waits bruised, broken, and vulnerable
along a curb washed in harsh brilliance.

The Hemingway organ's siren song,
and hieratic beat coaxing man along,
until ephemeral memories have gone.

The alarmed tourist now knows;
feels their approaching pursuers.
Must save himself, must escape.
Abandons woman, kids, and cats
to an illuminated bus stop shack.
It's over. Freedom. Free at last.
Don't run, act normal, just walk away.
An approaching dark form blocks his way,
then a chrome pistol's muzzle flash:

noise, pain, exhaustion, stagger, oblivion.

The Hemingway organ's siren song,
and hieratic beat coaxing man along,
until ephemeral memories have gone.

Fight to return, regain consciousness;
guided back by a refrain growing louder,
its beat stronger, inexorable.
Men on stools or standing at their bleak wood bar;
soaking in music, smoke, talk, and bluster.
The pungent, spindly vagabond specter
with unkempt, stubble beard
smiling at the bar's far end
raises a half-full whiskey glass
to the addled tourist, now one of them;
newfound friend or another back again.

The Hemingway organ's siren song,
and hieratic beat coaxing man along,
until ephemeral memories have gone.

Through a Wyrd Portal

Creation's eternal muse, lord, and master,
past, present, and forever.
Ineffable and ubiquitous Wyrd,
surpassing gods, science, and nature.

The unkempt tourist;
a seeker in clogs and haircloth
embracing this unknown course
for instant, hour, day, or eternity.
Climbing the circular staircase,
turning ever right, moving ever upward;
shouldering an unwieldy bag
through the somber candlelit passage,
until an ethereal glow reveals his room.

The chosen portal;
only one of those innumerable:
disease, fasting, pain, drugs, ritual,
insanity, Sun Dance, the hundred cuts.
Its entrance token, a carved cypress box
guiding entry to this mythical chamber;
pulled from the moisture-darkened crotch
of a single, deep-rooted primeval tree
standing stark in some forest clearing,
growing strong, apart, and shrouded in bittersweet perfume.

The dark, bleak door
swinging partly ajar;
threatening, beckoning, cautioning;
its primordial pull paralyzing flight.
Hesitant twist on tarnished brass knob.

A solitary flickering candle
in a windowless turret room.
One entrance, no windows, no corners;
stark, barren, still, close, constricting;
a gratuitous space created for ornamentation,
pregnant with anxious anticipation;
portal to mythical, unbounded vision,
beyond mere corporeal logic.

The expectant seeker
squats dead center recalling nothing, forgetting everything.
Singularity, aspiration, destination, and speech
compress to one existential place and moment.
A kit bag not his own, its mysterious contents holding all
to be recalled,
to be seen,
to be experienced,
to be survived.

The bottomless bag
disgorges straight-razor, incense, purple glass vial,
square dark blanket, and soothing powder.
Unconsciously, he drags and scrapes his scalp.
Straight razor shearing away hair
without pain, without marks.
Falling locks drift to the floor,
passing through worn cedar planks,
then, when set aside, his razor follows.

The wool blanket
unrolls at the nucleus;
absent color; neither glossy, flat, nor dull.
Only planets, stars, and galaxies above.
Touch, feel, grasp, and crawl
'til upending that ominous, deep blue vial.
Its spreading contents discoloring the floor,
as the toppled bottle sinks through dusty boards,
creating a widening, dull-purple stain.

The carved cypress box
emerging from this blanket,
lacks lock, hinge, or metal trim;
its sides and lid carved
with nature's scenes,
long-gone people and places;
bringing successive waves of emotion;
touching a past beyond this circular barrier;
soon obscured by an invasive, expanding cloud.

The reassuring haircloth tunic
unfastened and cast aside;
woven from source unknown.
Naked, powdered body
transforming to incorporeal;
feeling fresh, feeling clean.
Discarded garb and powder flask,
sink through thin, dusty boards
outside the dark blanket island.

The incense sticks
rubbed together; once, twice, thrice,
until subdued ignition.
Smoldering vapors curl up and away.
Stick butts are forced through blanket
into cracks between dusty boards.
Perfumed tendrils ascend through absent ceiling,
to an infinite, dark empyrean void.

The loves lost and vanished times
are shed; first one then another.
Absolute acceptance preceding Wyrd
as the darkening purple stain expands;
absorbing attention and consciousness,
inducing unendurable intensity.
Closed eyes refuse commands,
overwhelming fear, inextinguishable visions.

The tall, red-oak frame gallows

appears with its proud, black-hooded hangman
haltered and laughing on his own trap,
before tripping its lever release
to plunge through trailing the rope end.
A seeker peers down through that opening
into a windowless turret room;
sees himself sitting on the dark, wool blanket,
gaping at the spreading stain.
Apparition, reflection, image, or self?

The alarmed seeker
continues staring through the aperture,
dry tears leaving glistening tracks
down soothing off-white powder.
Leaning forward, reaching forward
before tumbling through that same eternal void,
hurtling through a dark chill,
flailing for the ungraspable;
an anchor, a handhold, a belief, a faith.
Forever plunging, terrified and screaming
through an endless fall without sense.

The cotton candy mist
envelops all, slows descent,
panic subsides, breathing ceases;
no discomfort for the phantom
cleaved from his corporeal form
to embark on a quintessence path beyond gods;
drawn towards its fountainhead.

The mortal spirit
dispersed and discarded
before encountering another;
vengeful, kind, and supreme;
beyond nature, animal, man, and gods;
undefined, unbounded, predominant.

The frail writhing form
enters this abyss without hesitation; without question.

Pulled through an aperture
of delirium and suffering
on the journey few take and fewer survive.
One that births myth, legend, and religion.
A chill breeze arrives absent direction,
raising to a maelstrom, subsiding to tenuous calm;
bringing false peace with unnerving visions
floating past a fine membrane
separating sanctuary from slaughter.

The disturbed seeker
stares through this obscuring film
to a spirit family at their bountiful table;
an insulated island without boundary.
Patriarch, matriarch, and progeny
intent on their feast insouciant.
Who will not clean their plate?
Who is getting attention?
Who will be absolved?
Who missed service?
Who was offending?
Who stumbled?
Who fell?
Who?

The continuously emerging scene
encircling this warm light and casual talk
offers a surreal, disparate, wretched tableau;
disconnected, unmoving, and ignored.
Darkness, ruin, and debris.
Soldier propped against a shattered wall,
bleeding out through dirty khaki.
A headless torso descending into churned mud;
Loud demented woman, pleading for man and child;
then more, many more; to the far horizon.

The sudden revulsion
overwhelming and repugnant;
cannot look away, cannot turn back,

pulled irresistibly towards what?
A spectral vision?
A place at the table?
A place beyond the table?
Another reality? To become forever insane?
What world? Whose world? A world at all?
The harsh rug chaffs his convulsing body;
sweat dampens this husk cleaved from its soul.

The anguish and despair
hesitantly recede in gentle waves;
an outgoing tide, seawater lapping warm sand,
until warmth returns, more sensed than sensate;
seducing, consuming, then overwhelming.
Impenetrable brightness; exhilarating beauty.
A meadow with green grass swaying gently,
one couple gazing into each other's eyes.
As they're approached, the girl moves smoothly,
and lovers gently clasp hands.
Two become three then many;
identities submerge in their sodality.

The impelling breeze
returns to caress senses,
gently swirling the cotton candy mist,
until the universe stills without notice.
Benign white turns damp, bitter gray;
clawing the psyche; parting to uncloak three figures.
A shrouded, searching necromancer,
probing misty banks with his shepherd's crook.
A determined woman with her young boy,
defending against some invisible presence's advance;
refusing to yield, resisting blows, refusing passage,
resisting what's ordained.
A mother and child grow more distinct;
her protected progeny happily shifts wood blocks.

The nebulous gray mist
darkens and thickens;

its impenetrable chill curtain
releasing a solitary, panicked figure;
running, face distorted, brow sheening.
He stumbles, tumbles, recovers then runs past.
A hysterical woman follows close behind;
bright-eyed, disheveled, unsteady,
screaming, raving, and staggering.
Behind these fugitives,
deep within this mist cloak,
a common, collective moan
pierced by inconsolable screams.
Mortal terror's fearful pitch and volume grows
as more emerge; fleeing this foul, gray shroud.

The demented runners
race past in spasmodic flight then vanish.
As this cacophony diminishes,
the mist becomes translucent before lifting;
leaving an endless azure sky;
temperate, pleasurable, unthreatening.
Infinity lies above this boundless, tawny plain;
its surface freckled by naked minions,
running aimlessly, avoiding, colliding,
tripping over illusory impediments.
Some sit upright, unmoving;
others curl into tight balls;
frozen, terrified, eyes clamped shut;
seeking the womb's warm sanctuary.
When one wraith senses another too close
sullen silence turns to screaming, oaths, threats.

The returning zephyr
gently lifts this seeker.
Borne up and away,
unnoticed by those left below
spawning and succoring hysteria.
Borne up and away,
with the warming mist-cloak
growing unbearable and suffocating.

Borne up and away,
sweating hard and profusely,
without dampness or sensation.
Borne up and away,
into increasing density, less translucence,
then impenetrable opaqueness.

The visceral view
from close above yet unseen;
imperfectly masked by height.
Looking down on the aristo and peasant's savage clash.
One stumbles and the other cuts, thrusts, hacks;
howling triumphant with each new gash.

The impotent seeker
seethes, screaming silently.
Must halt it, demand it stop, plead for an end.
Unable to persuade, unable to menace
absent will, weapon, power, or time;
until a gentle zephyr returns the cotton candy mist;
wet, pink, and crimson to cloak the mania below.

The frantic seeker
must withdraw, turn away,
escape madness, regain self-control,
live in pleasant, comfortable ignorance,
abandon this quest, quit this odyssey,
end this surreal sortie to seek Wyrd.
Life and living matter, this does not.
Nothing is on offer here for mortals.
Search elsewhere for reason.

The awakening seeker
must break away, must escape.
Comb the temporal, gods, faith, and science.
Flee, leave such apparitions to their reality.
Do not embrace, do not explore, do not enter;
accept eternal and infinite uncertainty,
acknowledge the undefinable.

The struggling seeker
resists his own momentum;
must return to the portal,
must return to the room,
must return to consciousness,
must recover life's gift.
What key, what course, what now?
Focus. Concentrate on the room;
that safe harbor, portal, mirage
an instant and eternity distant.
Concentrate on the tree;
natural, ancient, leafless,
gnarled roots driven deep in firm ground.

The refocusing seeker
struggles, frantic and desperate;
closing eyes, mind, soul, and senses.
Withdraw, withdraw, withdraw.
The momentum fades, slows, stops, and reverses.
Hold course, ignore evanescent sounds,
retreat past stars, visions, revelations, apparitions.
Resist exhaustion, numbness, and entreaties.
Tolerate no hesitation, no vacillation;
escape or endure a terrifying eternity.

The reemerging seeker
ignores all but the Wyrd tree,
imagining its trunk, feeling the moist mist,
sensing the gentle zephyr returning;
its increasing wind strong and warm.
Outstretched arms breach its cloak,
eyes open to harsh lightning flashes;
snow, gray sky, dreary winter clouds.
Meld with the large knothole wound
as a rising wind howls, screams, moans.

The resolute seeker
ignores all but its rough, moist bark,

grasps its texture, rasps his forehead.
Sensation returns. Crushed nose, bruised lips, sore limbs.
Fatigue drives away unnatural exuberance.
Human form regained; standing against the tree.
Fall's dead grass and roots scratch bare feet.
Arms clench the trunk, tears flood strained eyes.
An unsure hand grasps one bare shoulder;
his naked frame twists to face the first mortal.
Grasping desperately, unsuccessfully for this savior;
who bolts down some vaguely remembered path
along a narrow stream's soft bank,
past woodlot and pregnant meadow,
where suckers are speared on spring evenings,

The alighting seeker
senses and remembers
spring's damp, warming promise;
summer's dry heat, pleasant breezes and cooling storms;
fall's glorious transformation and festive warning;
winter's frozen ground, cloaked by each virgin snow.
Evening passes to night as the tree fades.
Concentrate on waking, fight to return;
convulsing between twisted bedcovers.

The recovering seeker
dreams strong and well;
walking through tall grass,
a summer meadow,
a stand of undulating trees,
a bird's throaty voice,
a grasshopper's whirl;
soft grass brushing cotton shorts.
Open windows bringing fresh outside air,
laden with spring, forcing out the stale and foul.

The awakening seeker
spies his carved cypress box
on the dresser, reflected in its mirror.
Staggering across his pleasant bedroom,

he lefts it gently then smashes the casket against a sill;
vanquish, crush, destroy.
Relief comes as this obliteration ends;
then snuggle under a warm, down comforter,
alive and satiated in a room growing cooler;
sleeping deep and strong.

The repatriated seeker
slumbers calm and peaceful
near a carved cypress box on marble-top dresser,
with brass lock, hinges, and trim;
with unremarkable scenes carved into sides and lid.
Holding trinkets of little value
except to this fading tourist and seeker no longer.

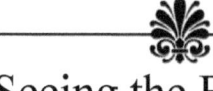

Seeing the Elephant

Crimson clouds, quivering and transfixed,
straining an orange sun's translucent beams
as night gives way to early morning stillness.
Hills and valleys erupt on the far horizon
beyond this broad plain's debris and putrid detritus;
flashing intermittent with disrupting brilliance;
illuminating bare adobe slopes and bald crests;
until a dull rumbling heralds the saturated plain's jelly tremble.
Each upheaval travels down a solitary, endless, rutted track
between skeletal trees scattered amongst this devastation;
empty citadels, shattered redoubts, and malevolent trenches.
A tourist staggers forward amid enmity's miserable chronicle.

Distant hills flash, glow, and shimmer
beyond mounds of fallen carpeting this plain;
soaking, sinking, settling into sodden ground;
their battered, broken, decaying cadavers
strewn along this dismal course and beyond.
Smashed chariots, discarded spears, swords,
breastplates, helmets, and shields;
jumbled amongst slings, bows, and other debris.
Hoplites, Immortals, soldiers, concubines, innocents;
white, brown, black, yellow descend into rapacious mud;
defiled by time, animals, and avian scavengers.

Forward; whatever course the Gods decree,
open leather sandals cut deep in sore, swollen skin;
batter-mud oozing between raw toes resisting each step.
Bronze shield strapped to aching arm and hand;
the other clutching an obdurate spear.
Leather greaves and ponderous bronze breastplate;
helmet and gloves long since discarded;

tired, wet, solitary, and trembling;
with fallen comrades left behind,
on the road from Thermopylae.

Dank gray mist blankets morning's putrid field,
in the surreal aura shrouding a relentless sun;
distant foothills' spasmodic flashing,
saturated earth quivering to successive dull shocks;
rousting the plain traversed by one furrowed track
spanning eight-hundred years' desolation.
A disfigured domain marked by skeletal trees
rising amongst decaying horses and humans
amidst maces, arrows, battle axes, lances,
great swords, arbalests, and longbows.
Slaughtered horses, harnessed to derelict carts and wagons,
forever denied their crenelated granite shelters,
lay silent and impotent below towering trebuchets.

Forward, then forward, soldier of devout legions;
swathed in smothering tunic and surcoat,
wearing quilt chausses, aketon, and hauberk;
burdened by unforgiving linked mail,
heavy and dull under belted surcoat.
Once proud, now threadbare embroidery;
dulled by steel mittens grasping a crushing broadsword.
Rough cloth cap bedding simple, unadorned iron helm.
Breathing comes hard and speech inconceivable
in the narrow world visible through an occularium.
Sweltering dampness impregnating lambequin and cape.
Place one booted foot forward, then drag the other,
forward and drag, forward and drag;
endless fatigue, through a torrid desert,
and no return once on Jerusalem's road.

Midmorning's sweet-smelling decomposition,
intensifies a plain strewn with endless desolation
and untold shattered remains.
Less bright flashes bathe far hills and adobe ravines;
their menace flooding over a staggering tourist

as the relentless sun rises towards its zenith
above surreal fields once pregnant with crops;
now purgatory's realm, field, and miasma.

Forward, forward, then forward
through midday's steaming closeness,
staggering without complaint;
weary, keen, and loyally resolute.
Cocooned in brilliant five-color armor,
lacquered leather, and black metal.
Crushing weight, rigid and unwieldy,
the armored horse long-since down,
plumed helmet compressing head;
unreachable sweat seeping slowly
between skin and padding
but no retreat on the Zhongdu road.

Sullied clouds borne lightly above the plain,
with the slightest zephyr caressing its dead;
obscuring that immutable track's vanishing point,
far beyond a column of the weary and faceless.
Broken men, old men, hollow-eyed women,
disoriented, defenseless children with bloated bellies
in desperate, wretched flight from those flashing hills;
a centipede stumbling hesitatingly towards the tourist,
slowly coming nearer, nearer, nearer, and nearer.
Shuffling past, apathetic, unstoppable;
their low, wailing dirge finally fading to silence.

Flash, dark, flash; as dusky afternoon descends
softening crests, peaks, ridges, and valleys.
Snow carpets debris, detritus, and devastated remains.
Men, horses harnessed to caissons, broken-wheeled cannons,
sabers, muskets, and rifles share frozen ground with lance and saber;
stiffening in winter's frigid embrace outside Vauban's walled city.
Starving, frostbitten, abandoned, exhausted
one foot forward then the next, the next, and the next;
slowly lurching blindly away from a numbing, killing ground.
Liberty, equality, fraternity long since discarded and forgotten;

abandoned amongst those left frozen along the track.
All fervor crushed, or discarded; with Imperial Eagles.

Forward, forward, forward, and forward to sanctuary;
killed and harried by winter's avenging wind
cutting through multi-colored uniform remnants;
residuum of a once auspicious blooming;
that gay bouquet of carabiners, cuirassiers, dragons,
lancers, hussars, chasseurs, horse artillery, grenadiers,
fusiliers, engineers, and their ample trains.
Thinning greatcoats, packs and shakos left to scavengers,
vanishing boots, windburned faces, unsteady legs,
gray-white blackened feet, hands, and ears;
splitting skin, throbbing with pain, going numb;
wrapped in uniform cloth stripped from the dead.
Clinging to a useless musket and stained bayonet,
dragging limbs near collapse with overwhelming fatigue;
struggling to endure the tortured road from Moscow.

Sultry late afternoon dulls distant flashing hills,
beyond ravaged fields, orchards, rivers, and trees;
laying fallow except for war's inexorable detritus
borne of an interminable, loathsome summer.
Brother war in a bountiful land pregnant with hate;
poisoned by architects ever absent from this field;
their virtuous cause's tariff avoided through bounty.
The reluctant forced to serve, to defend, to charge;
then join expiring men, women, and children.
Honor fades amidst broken standards,
shattered cannons surround the tourist,
darkening visions of glorious victory.

Forward, forward, forward, forward, ever forward,
bereft of army, brigade, regiment, or battalion.
Loyalty, allegiance, cause?
For whom, for what, and why?
Exhausted, footsore, famished,
kepis and slouch hat discarded,
shoe leather cracked, disintegrating pasteboard soles,

colorless uniforms frayed and threadbare;
all else cast-off, dropped aside, left behind;
but the un-blued rifle kept clean and oiled
with ready caps and cartridges;
route marching along Petersburg pike

Rolling flashes, rumbling dull thunder into evening;
far beyond clinging mud and collapsing trenches,
lifeless shell-ponds, and coiling barbed wire.
Destroyed field pieces, steel shields punctured;
crumpled canvas bird with empennage angled skyward,
stubby nose deep in mud, and lifeless arm draped alongside.
An indifferent natural world's resilient red poppies rising
from churned ground between wet, wretched redoubts.
Approaching column of benign, sightless soldiers;
war brothers in dirty khaki, horizon blue, or field gray;
sightless under filthy wet cloth bandaging,
unknowing who their single hand grasps ahead.
led by their single, seeing sergeant;
blood seeping through his dirty sling.
Broken and faceless; hollow colorless eyes,
a disconsolate human millipede,
stumbling nearer, nearer, nearer, and nearer,
down the furrowed track before passing.
Their wretched future repulsing the tourist;
who turns away, unable to follow, unwilling to look;
even after their shuffling tread and rattling breaths fade.

Forward, forward, forward, forward, forward, forward
comrades, subjects, serfs, citizens, patriots,
giving their last measure to end all wars.
Fifty-thousand hopes, dreams, and lives
walk into consuming machine guns,
collapsing into late afternoon mud.
Magazine rifle clicks against steel helmet,
pressing down head and shoulders,
wet feet rotting in low-topped boots,
saturated leggings, puttees, and clothing;
leather harnesses constrain sunken chests;

shell shock, trench foot, and influenza.
Days of survival, days of agony, days of death;
their vision immutably fixed at five-hundred meters,
every hope of existence cradled in one steel notch;
cursing the insane road to Passchendaele.

Flashes are clearer, twilight's noise more thunderous;
a horseman gallops steadily down the furrowed track,
hooves spraying mud, curved saber uplifted, thrust forward,
a winged helmet phantom parting misery's surreal miasma,
outthrust abused breastplate, dirty red cape trailing aloft.

Forward, forward, and forever forward.
His black charger's nostrils flare, pulse, drip;
darkening flanks, mouth foaming, eyes flashing.
The death's-head relentless, galloping approach,
urged on by righteousness, fear, hate, anger, and more;
thundering towards a nauseous tourist.
Closer and closer; must be met; must be stopped;
time to stand; no escape, no flight, no retreat.

Desperate and determined, the tourist casts about;
grasping a steel-tipped lance from resisting mud.
Butt planted in ground, spearpoint angled up and forward;
horse or rider, rider or horse, horse or rider?
Can't recall answer. Terror, fear, resolve.
Nearer, nearer, nearer, nearer, and nearer;
ignore the saber, shut eyes, resist hysteria,
close the mind; cast aside pointless morals;
must not run, must stand, must not yield.

Shock, crash, cries, then blindness.
The elephant seen, felt, met, embraced;
as night descends on this desolate plain.
Tourist no longer; a survivor, a perpetuator
astride his black charger, hurtling down the track
galloping hard, mud splashing,
grasping a heavy curved saber,
sweating hands tired, weary,

watching the approaching figure far ahead;
walking cautiously up the rutted track,
approaching the flashing adobe hills;
some probing, unarmed successor.

Acquiescence

Flitting visions of events long past,
fantasy's ghosts, family spirits,
phantom friends, enemy specters.
Illusions of other times;
memories of place, joy, sorrow.

Accept a lifetime's profusion;
whether reality, lie, or phantasm.
Let it slip, let it pass, let it go;
embrace the inevitable, the unknown;
join one's welcoming ghosts;
as will those soon left behind.

At the Precipice

Yesterdays slip to an eternal void
between night and morning.
Today's half over by noon;
gone forever, irretrievable,
except muddled memories.
What is turns unceasingly to what was,
as foregone futures flash past;
easy, peaceful, difficult,
painful, terrifying, hopeful.
Approaching visions, narrow and fleeting,
abandon the past to those left behind;
leaving the future to our gods.

Crossing the Styx

That uncharted river,
from source unknown,
with one familiar shore.

That unmarked landing,
nexus for every soul's road
and every journey's end;
whether in ignorance, resignation,
fear, terror, pain, or bliss.

That tariff surrendered
for an inescapable crossing,
then down an unseen path,
traveled by all, feared by some,
welcomed by others.

That unfathomable passage,
revealed to those entering,
and before then not at all.
Disquieting without true faith
or some ruthless final weighing with;
but inescapable when summoned.

Homage to a Line

Monuments tightly cast over a flowing field
smelling of fresh-mown spring grass;
dull and polished, stone or marble;
tall, short, ornate, simple, and flat.
Resisting sun, snow, wind, and rain.
Marking lives lived well, poorly, or hardly at all;
unremembered pleasure, poverty, wealth, and pain
under silent, cloaking sod.

A pleasant setting, quiet and peaceful,
alongside town and bending, joyous stream;
all carefully tended, manicured, protected,
over generations.

No diminutive family cemetery,
amidst farms on some gravel road;
shielded by wood and wire fences;
open to trespass by those unworthy.
Weathered stones obscured by uncut grass;
or overturned near its surrounding cornfield.

No stark, melancholy state home cemetery,
with efficient, convenient, numbered graves,
buried and forgotten amidst encroaching grass.

No regimented, overseas cemetery;
beside lines of comrades left behind
in neat rows with chiseled name or question.

Grandma Jeep and Grandma Buick,
leave home with shared grandsons,
in the sculptured Lincoln Premiere;

from the doctor's white Victorian house
across an oiled alley behind main street.
Past the Second Ward School
perched on the long sledding hill
behind city hall and funeral home.

Their progeny soon race with wondrous abandon,
down the nursery's pungent, harlequin rows
with blooming plants of many gay colors;
under a vented glass roof's humid heat;
courtesy of a thousand green panes
filtering spring's warming sun.

Through the welcoming cemetery portal;
stone gateposts severing a wrought-iron fence.
Driving slow and silent down sandy path-roads
edged by the gentle, green grass mat,
curving around low, serene hills
past cement, granite, and stone monuments;
large, small, flat and tall;
interspersed with family crypts
and long-handled, red water hydrants.
Tranquility achieved below chirping birds
gliding between oaks and maples.

Released from the rear seat's hot, clinging plastic;
their grandchildren scatter, scampering happily
over the dead and between curious markers;
afraid to lose sight of two grandmothers
lifting geraniums from an open trunk
where wooden flats traveled beside a spare tire;
alongside gay pansies to ring the house.

Running undaunted beneath a bright sun,
around oblong dirt patches without grass,
avoiding swiveling lawn sprinklers' streams,
reading carved names, dashes, and dates;
wondering what lies beneath settling ground.
While grandmothers clear, clean, plant, water,

and reminisce of past worlds below;
while the boys' run and play exuberantly overhead;
leaving buried ancestors to the unknown.

In time, the women have joined those they tend,
an old man returns; walking slowly among
forgotten forebears, family, and friends.
Each passing through the granite portal,
from sickness, accident, war, or wear;
their stories told, remembered, lost, transformed.
Two loving grandmothers, not yet forgotten,
haunt such thoughts; but there are no children.
The last of four families surveys
these pleasant grounds and awaits their embrace.

About the Author

Michael T. Ribble was born in Lapeer, Michigan, then moved to Davison during early grade school and completed high school there. His family left for Colorado after residing at several locations in both cities and nearby farms. Prior to enlisting in the navy he was employed at road construction, farmed, was a camp counselor, worked cattle, pumped gas, harvested sugar beets, helped build a feedlot, and was a college parking lot attendant. While in the navy, he finished basic training and spent a year at Guantanamo Bay, Cuba, before entering officer candidate school. His active and reserve assignments before retiring as captain include a cruiser, destroyer, frigate, and two minesweepers.

Mr. Ribble studied at University of Colorado in Boulder and received a bachelor's degree in journalism from Central Michigan University. He holds a Master of Business Administration degree from Florida State University and completed the United States Naval War College's continuing education program. While an undergraduate he assisted teaching a journalism lecture course and on active duty taught naval science as an assistant professor at Northwestern University. He has held program management, integrated logistics support, and cost estimating positions at Naval Sea Systems Command and the Department of Homeland Security. Besides completing four Lieutenant Jacob Starke novels his work has appeared in university publications, newspapers, and U.S. Naval Institute *Proceedings*.

www.ingramcontent.com/pod-product-compliance
Lightning Source LLC
Chambersburg PA
CBHW060357080526
44583CB00012B/350